Deliciously Corrupt:

A Satirical Food and Cocktail Guide to the Roberts Supreme Court

If you think that climate change is a hoax, government should control women's bodies and reproductive rights, guns have more rights than people, a former president can overturn the will of the people and foment an insurrection, rich guys can buy elections, corporations and the wealthiest shouldn't pay taxes, or if you simply don't believe in democracy, then this cookbook isn't for you!

Acknowledgements

A special thank you to: Dan, Elisa, Glen, Joe, Kate, Maddy, Mark, Marty, Sandy, Erica, Lorraine, and my wonderful mother, Shirley, who I miss every day, and a heartfelt thank you and shout-out to the Supreme Court for doing everything in their power to make this cookbook a best seller!

This cookbook combines all my favorite things: cooking, politics, ranting, humor, cynicism, and sarcasm. It's been a fun project!

Who Are These Guys?

The recipe titles in this cookbook are how I imagine the Supreme Court Justices (or at least six of them) would compile a charity or community cookbook, like so many charities and churches do every year. Yes, the titles may be sarcastic, but the recipes are tasty!

This is a cookbook and personal primer that serves up the John Roberts Supreme Court with a heaping side of humor and sarcasm. You can take it with a giant grain of your favorite sea salt but be warned: six men and women on an out-of-control, unrestrained, untethered, ideology-over-law, conservative court currently control our country's fate. The only ones who can stop them are us, and the only way to do that is by voting.

So, let's see what the conservatives on John Roberts' Supreme Court have done for America. They brought us *Citizens United v. FEC* ... you remember, the ruling that found corporations are people when it comes to spending endless amounts of money on their favored political outcomes, but not when it comes to paying taxes. How's that working for you?

Despite an epidemic of gun violence that does not occur in any other first world country, this court continues to rule that a gun's right to kill supersedes your - and your children's – right to live. It's just that simple. How's that working for you?

Women have less rights than a group of dividing cells made by a fertilized egg. Less rights than an embryo. No treatment for a deadly ectopic pregnancy; no way to end a pregnancy that is created out of rape or incest; no right to terminate a pregnancy for a nonviable fetus, not even to save the life of the mother; and no remedy to end a pregnancy that you don't want, can't afford, or can't manage. They want to deny a woman the dignity to decide what is best for her and her health. What century are we in? How's that working for you?

For decades, this court has consistently put corporate profits above common-sense laws that could help mitigate climate change that scientists are now saying may be too late to control. How's that working for you?

Who are these activist judges and how can they get away with it? In most cases they have moved beyond partisanship, often flying in the face of settled law, decency, or public opinion in favor of legislating their agendas from the bench, foisting conservative dogma on us without a shred of oversight. Several of them blatantly lied under oath during their confirmation hearings when they said *Roe v. Wade* was settled case law. How can any court in the United States wield so much uncontested power? This is governing by fiat.

During the next presidential election, please throw away your purity tests and never forget that when you vote, you are choosing a President who will nominate any Supreme Court vacancies occurring during his or her term (well, unless you are Obama), and depending on whom they appoint, there is the potential for reprehensible consequences that can last for decades.

Remember when George W. Bush was running for president in 2000? He was touted as 'the guy you'd want to have a beer with!' You didn't get the beer, instead, you got Sam Alito. Eighteen years later, how's that working for you? Just when you thought it can't get any worse…Can you imagine the next 40 years with Supreme Court Justice Aileen Cannon?

Alito said, "One side is going to win." They're not even trying to hide the fact that the fix is in. Deliciously corrupt, indeed. When the referees are working for only one team, we are in terrible trouble. Please remember this when you vote in November

I hope you get a laugh, enjoy the recipes, and have a good meal! You can reach me at deliciouslycorrupt@gmail.com

DD

Photographs by TingeyInjuryLawFirm, Katrin Hauf, and Ian Hutchinson on Unsplash

Table of Contents

APPETIZERS

Game Day Dip (Roberts Only Calls 'Balls and Strikes')

And if you believe that...you're an idiot!

Ingredients

- 1 can Fritos Bean Dip
- 1 package taco seasoning
- 1 bunch scallions
- 3 oz cream cheese
- 8 oz sour cream
- 1 lb. shredded cheddar cheese

Cooking Steps

Mix all ingredients and heat until bubbly. Serve hot with tortilla chips or Fritos Scoops.

Brie with Curry and Chutney (Upholding Rich, White University Legacies)

Delicious served with chilled Chardonnay that doesn't have a screw top! A favorite of rich alumni everywhere!

Ingredients

- 1 medium wheel of brie
- Curry powder
- Major Grey's Chutney (Crosse & Blackwell or Patak's because they are easy to find and not too over-the-top with multiple ingredients)
- Chopped cashews (raw or roasted)

Cooking Steps

Heat the oven to 400F degrees. Use a 10 oz to 15 oz wheel of brie. It can be larger, just adjust the ingredients. (I use the 13.4 oz Kirkland brand from Costco). Pat a lot of curry powder on both sides and roll the edges in the curry powder that rolls off. I use a lot of curry powder because I like curry. Put the brie on a small cookie sheet. I use the toaster oven tray and cook it in the toaster oven, but a regular oven is fine. Use about 6 oz or about a half a jar of the chutney (a little less or more won't matter) and smooth on top of the curried brie. Try and keep it on the top of the brie, but it won't particularly matter if it runs a little. Sprinkle the chopped cashews (I use about a medium fistful, not all that many) on top of the brie.

Bake until the cheese starts to melt onto the pan. Serve immediately with crackers or a sliced French baguette. Extremely easy and always popular.

Beluga Caviar on Ice with Toast Points and Condiments (Private Yachts, Only)

Bummer! Beluga caviar is illegal to sell in the US because Beluga sturgeon has been overfished and is now on the endangered species list. So, if you want to eat like a Supreme Court Justice, you'll need to be on a yacht outside US waters, just like the Justices.

Ingredients

- 1 loaf of thin sliced bread
- 1/2 cup butter
- 1 tin Ossetra or Sevruga caviar – or any substitute you like and can afford! Allow 1 oz of caviar per person and gauge your garnishes accordingly.
- Finely chopped hard-cooked eggs, whites and yolks are kept separate.
- Crème fraiche
- Diced red onion
- Lemon wedges

Cooking Steps

Trim the crusts and slice in half on the diagonal, twice, to form four triangles. Butter lightly and place the bread in a single layer on a baking sheet. Bake the bread in a preheated 350F degree oven for 8 to 10 minutes, checking to make sure it does not become too dark. Cool the toast points on a baking rack. Serve with caviar (or keep for a day in an airtight container). Put the caviar tin on top of a bed of crushed ice, and serve it with a bone, mother-of-pearl, gold-plated, or even a plastic spoon. Do not use silver or stainless steel; both caviar and spoon will suffer. Place it on a tray with garnishes of your choice. Keep the caviar tin in the coldest part of your refrigerator until about a half-hour before serving (heat and oxygen are caviar's biggest enemies.)

Chili Con Queso Mexicano (Border Town Classic)

What makes border towns really special? Delicious food!

Ingredients

- 6 fresh chilies, roasted, peeled, and cut in lengthwise slices (Hatch chilies or poblano or if you like it hot, maybe 1 jalapeño)
- 1 onion, chopped
- 2 T bacon grease
- 1 clove garlic, minced
- 2 large fresh tomatoes, peeled and finely chopped
- 2 1/2 cups grated jack or cheddar cheese (or combo of both cheddar and jack)
- Salt to taste

Cooking Steps

First, you will need to roast the chiles. Place the chiles under the broiler or on the burner if you have gas, until blackened, about 5 minutes per side. Really char them. Place the chiles in a paper sack or plastic food-storage bag, close it tightly and let the chiles steam for 20 minutes. Take the chiles out of the bag and gently rub off the skin. Remove the stem and seeds, then slice the chiles from top to bottom to open them up. (We remove the seeds).

Sauté the chilies and onion in the bacon grease. Then add garlic and cook until soft. Add the remaining ingredients and heat until the cheese melts, stirring often. Serve hot with tortilla chips.

Shrimp Cocktail (An Alito Fishing Trip Must-Have)

If you want to live like a Supreme Court Justice, substitute lobster like the big boys do!

Ingredients

- 1 lb. shelled, deveined, large shrimp, cooked, cooled, and cut into three or four pieces depending on the size
- 1 cup seeded and diced English cucumber
- 1 cup (about 6 oz) seeded and halved green grapes
- 2 large scallions, thinly sliced, (light green and white parts only)
- 1/4 cup diced red onion
- 1 medium jalapeño or serrano chili pepper, seeded, and finely chopped
- 1/2 cup fresh lime juice
- 1/4 tsp kosher salt
- 1/2 cup fresh cilantro leaves
- 1 medium avocado
- Salt to taste

Cooking Steps

Transfer the cooled shrimp to a large bowl and add the cucumber, grapes, scallions, red onions, and jalapeño.

Season with the lime juice and salt and toss to combine.
Cover and refrigerate for 1 hour. Add the cilantro and
avocado just before serving and toss to combine. Serve cold
in individual short/medium size cocktail glasses so you can
show off the colorful shrimp cocktail. Serves 4.

Salmon Avocado Sushi Boats with Salmon Roe Garnish (Rethink Roe? No!)

Not a chance, no way, no how! The 69% of Americans (CNN poll) who disagree with overturning Roe are S.O.L.

Ingredients

- 1 1⁄4 cups water
- 3 T rice vinegar
- 2 tsp sugar
- 1⁄2 tsp salt
- 1 medium English cucumber
- 3 oz package cold-smoked salmon
- 1 avocado, thinly sliced
- 1 tsp black and/or white sesame seeds
- Small tin of salmon roe
- Condiment options: soy sauce, furikake rice seasoning,
- Kewpie mayonnaise, prepared wasabi, and/or pickled ginger, for serving

Cooking Steps

Rinse rice in a sieve under cold water until the water runs clear for about one minute. Bring the rice and water to a boil over medium-high heat in a saucepan. Reduce heat to medium; simmer covered until rice is tender and water is absorbed, about 15 minutes.

Meanwhile, whisk together vinegar, sugar, and salt in a small bowl until sugar and salt dissolve. Drizzle vinegar mixture over hot rice and gently fold together. Cover the surface of the rice with a damp paper towel; let cool to room temperature, about 1 hour.

Halve cucumbers lengthwise, then cut each half crosswise into four equal pieces (for a total of 16 pieces). Trim a thin slice from the peel side of each piece (so the pieces will sit flat). Scoop out seeds from each piece, leaving a 1/3-inch border. Spoon 1 to 1 1/2 T rice into each cucumber piece, then use damp hands to compact the rice. Top each with salmon and avocado.

Sprinkle with sesame seeds. Garnish with a sprinkling of salmon roe. Serve with soy sauce, furikake, Kewpie mayonnaise, wasabi, and/or ginger.

Recipe from *Allrecipes.com* (with my addition of salmon roe garnish).

Affogato Martini (To Celebrate Our Supreme Court Sovereignty)

Eye roll!

Ingredients

- 3 oz vodka, bourbon, or rum
- 2 oz freshly brewed espresso, cooled to room temperature
- 1 oz amaro (an Italian liqueur readily available in liquor stores)
- 2 oz coffee liqueur (look for a real coffee liqueur; you can use Kahlua, but it will be sweeter) (see note 1, below)
- 1 oz brown sugar syrup (see note 2, below)
- 2 scoops vanilla bean gelato (salted caramel gelato, chocolate gelato, or coffee gelato will work with this affogato martini recipe. Ice cream will absolutely work, too.)
- 6 espresso beans for garnish

Mixing Steps

Combine your spirit of choice, chilled espresso, amaro, coffee liqueur, and brown sugar syrup in a cocktail shaker. Fill the shaker halfway with ice and shake for 20 to 30 seconds until the shaker is too cold to handle.

Strain the chilled cocktail directly into two chilled coupe glasses (a stemmed cocktail glass with a rounded bowl with straight sides), then place a scoop of gelato into each glass. Garnish each with three espresso beans. Serves 2.

Note 1: Mr. Black or Forthave "Brown" are recommended brands of coffee liqueur.

Note 2: Brown sugar syrup. Put a 1/2 cup of brown sugar and water in a small sauce over medium heat. Stir the sugar and water together until the sugar is dissolved. Remove from the heat and let the syrup cool to room temperature. Leftover brown sugar syrup is wonderful in iced coffee.

Recipe from *A Flavor Journal.*

Bahama Mama Cocktails (Brett's High School Beach Week Tradition)

Look out, ladies! The boys are back in town.

Ingredients

- 2 cups crushed ice
- 2 oz orange juice
- 2 oz pineapple juice
- 1 oz dark rum
- 1 oz coconut-flavored rum
- 1 oz lime juice
- 1 oz grenadine syrup

Mixing Steps

In a blender, combine crushed ice, orange juice, pineapple juice (or Dole Orange Pineapple Banana Juice), regular rum, coconut-flavored rum, and grenadine. Blend until slushy. In honor of his 'Honor' Brett, you can add a dark rum floater for a little extra booze. Serves 2.

Champagne Cocktail (To Toast Donald for Making the Abortion Ban a Reality)

"His judges," as Trump likes to call them, thank him for stacking the court!

Ingredients

- 1 sugar cube
- 4 dashes of Angostura bitters
- Chilled champagne
- Lemon Twist

Mixing Steps

Add a sugar cube to the bottom of a champagne glass and add 4 dashes angostura bitters on top of the sugar cube.

Fill the glass with champagne or other sparkling wine. Garnish with a lemon twist.

Dirty Martini (The Drink for Weakening Clean Waterways)

Sorry kids, it's just a little toxic microplastic chemicals, along with corporation's waste and chemicals dumped into our rivers. Buck up, water doesn't catch on fire that often...

Ingredients

- 5 oz gin or vodka
- 1 oz dry vermouth
- 1 oz olive brine
- 4 to 6 olives

Mixing Steps

Add the gin or vodka, vermouth, and olive brine to a shaker filled with ice. Shake for 15 to 20 seconds until well chilled.

Double strain through a fine mesh strainer into two chilled martini glasses. Garnish with a skewer of olives. Serves 2.

Dobbs Cocktail ("Women are Witches:" Alito Cites 17th Century Misogynist to 'Mansplain' Dobbs Ruling)

Sam Alito, the 'Mansplainer' in Chief,' is driving women all over the country to drink - sometimes alone - so have enough of these Dobbs cocktails and you will forget how the Supreme Court screwed you!

Ingredients

- Add ice to a glass
- 3 oz gin
- 3 oz sweet vermouth
- 1 oz Fernet-Branca

Mixing Steps

Strain into two cocktail glasses and add a cherry.

Fernet-Branca is an Italian brand of fernet, a style of amaro or bitters. It was formulated in Milan in 1845 and is manufactured there by Fratelli Branca. Serves 2.

Ginni Tonic (With Just a Twist of Insurrection)

Ginni Thomas' favorite roadie when she's cruisin' in the RV with her "best friend," who she never 'talks to' about her lucrative political action work, texts, or opinions on elections and insurrections.

Ingredients

- 4 oz gin
- 6 oz tonic water
- Lime Wheels or any other seasonal garnishes you may prefer

Mixing Steps

Fill two glasses with ice, then add the gin. Add the tonic water and gently stir with a rolled-up crisp "gifted" $100 dollar bill.

Garnish with lime slices or lemon slices. Serves 2.

Lava Flow Cocktail (Keeps that Beautiful Citizens United Cash Spewing)

Like Mt. Vesuvius gushing money!

Ingredients

- 4 oz frozen strawberries
- 2 oz light run
- 2 oz coconut rum (you can use light rum if you don't have coconut rum)
- 2 small bananas
- 4 oz cream of coconut
- 4 oz pineapple juice
- 2 cups ice

Mixing Steps

Add strawberries, light rum, and coconut rum to a blender. Blend until combined. Pour mixture into two glasses and set aside. Rinse out the blender.

Now add banana, coconut cream, pineapple juice, and ice to the blender. Blend until well combined. Slowly pour the banana mixture over the strawberry mixture. Garnish with pineapple wedges.

This tropical drink is beautiful. Serves 2.

Limoncello Spritzer (The Supreme Court Official 'Golden Showers' Cocktail)

Fun and Exhilarating! Wee! Wee! Or if you are French speaking, Oui! Oui! (The Justices got the good idea from you know who!)

Ingredients

- 6 oz prosecco
- 4 oz limoncello
- 2 oz soda water

Mixing Steps

Add ice to two glasses. Divide the prosecco, limoncello, and soda water into two glasses. Give each glass a squeeze of fresh lemon juice and stir.

Garnish with lemon slices and fresh mint. Serves 2.

Recipe: Glen

Hand-Made-In Margarita (A Mainstay in Mrs. Coney Barrett's Household)

A Stepford Wife's guilty pleasure!

Ingredients

- 12 oz can limeade (Minute Maid in the freezer section next to frozen OJ)
- 12 oz empty can of limeade filled with tequila (you do not need the highest quality tequila: Costco tequila is fine for this recipe)
- 12 oz cold beer (not a lite beer)
- Lots of ice
- Lime
- Margarita Salt

Mixing Steps

Rim the lip of the glass with a lime and dip in the margarita salt. Empty the limeade into a blender. Fill the empty limeade can with tequila and pour it into the blender. Pour the 12 oz beer into the blender. Blend, and then add lots of ice. Blend until slushy. Pour the margaritas into glasses and serve immediately. After this you will never try another Margarita recipe.

If you use the giant limeade can, fill that giant empty can with tequila. One to one ratio between the limeade and tequila. Absurdly simple and delicious Margarita. It's a pitcherful.

Orange Russian Cocktail (For Putin's Prized Puppet – Strings Attached)

Some members of the Court are Pootie Poot fanboys too! He does it the Supreme Court's way; he rigs court cases and ignores laws that don't suit him.

Ingredients

- 2 oz Kahlua
- 2 oz orange vodka (see note)
- 2 oz heavy cream or half and half
- 1 dash orange bitters (optional)
- 2 orange peels for garnish

Mixing Steps

Put the Kahlua, orange vodka, and 1 dash of the orange bitters into cocktail shaker and fill with ice. Shake until well mixed and the liquid is cold. Pour into two glasses with ice and float half the cream on top of each glass. Garnish with orange peels. Serves 2.

Note: Look for either Ketel One Oranje Vodka or Absolut Mandarin Orange Vodka.

Recipe: Glen

Running Out of Thyme Cocktail (Climate Change is a Hoax! Oil Profits are Real!)

Just what you need when you realize that climate change is real and happening faster than you thought, and you know that the world is doomed. This refreshing drink will lift your spirits!

Ingredients

- 2 oz limoncello
- 2 oz gin
- Soda water
- Ice
- 2 sprigs of fresh thyme
- 2 lemon slices

Mixing Steps

Fill two glasses with ice and pour 1/2 the limoncello and 1/2 the gin into each glass. Fill each glass to the top with soda and garnish with a sprig of thyme and a lemon slice. Serves 2.

Cabbage and Cheese Soup (Ignore the Stench – We Certainly Do!)

"Supreme Court Stench," Sonia Sotomayor's on the money quote! This is a wonderful soup on a chilly night.

Ingredients

- 1 loaf French bread
- 1 head savoy or green cabbage
- 1 lb. fontina cheese, thinly sliced
- 1 cup grated parmesan cheese
- 4 to 5 oz pancetta or bacon chopped
- 2 quarts beef broth

Cooking Steps

Heat the oven to 375F degrees. Cut the bread into 1/4-inch slices. Core the cabbage and thinly slice. In an 8-quart pan, layer 1/3 each of the bread, cabbage, and fontina. Repeat with two more layers. Using your palms, press the layers until they are level.

Cook the pancetta over medium heat until crispy and drain the grease. Sprinkle the pancetta over the layers in the pan. In the same pan discard the fat, pour in the broth, bring to a boil, and pour over the layered ingredients.

Cover the pan tightly with a lid or tin foil. The mixture will puff up and the cheese will stick to the lid if it touches it. Bake 1 1/2 hours. Serves 4.

Chicken, Sausage, and Barley Soup (Cures Voter Suppression Depression)

Comfort food for the inevitable depression.

Ingredients

- 1 lb. Italian sausage (half mild and half hot sausage)
- 1 onion, chopped
- 3 cloves garlic, minced
- 3 large chicken breast halves (bone-in)
- 12-16 cups low sodium chicken broth (depends on how thick you like your soup…maybe more)
- 1 cup uncooked lentils
- 1 cup uncooked pearl barley
- 15 oz can garbanzo beans
- 12 oz bottle or container mild to medium salsa
- 1 lb. fresh spinach, washed

Cooking Steps

Remove sausage casings and crumble meat in a 5 to 6-quart pan over medium-high heat. Stir often until the meat is cooked. Drain off excess fat. Add the onion and garlic. Cook the onion until it is softened.

Add broth, chicken, barley, and lentils. Bring to a boil, cover, and simmer until the chicken breasts are cooked for about 30 minutes. Carefully remove the chicken (trying to not to remove too many lentils or barley, although you can return any to the pan with the chicken) and let cool. Discard skin and bones, shred chicken meat, and return to the pan. This recipe also works with meat from a rotisserie chicken. Pull the meat off the rotisserie chicken and add to the pan (skip cooking and adding the meat from the 3 breast halves if you use a rotisserie chicken).

Drain garbanzo beans and add to soup along with the salsa. Heat to a simmer and cook until the lentils and barley are tender (about another 30 minutes).

Add spinach and stir into soup and cook until the spinach is done. Ladle soup into bowls.

It freezes beautifully, so if you have any left, or make extra, no worries, it will be just as good. Serves 4 to 6.

Green Chili Soup (Because We're Really Chilly on Green Energy)

Piss off their corporate masters? They'll never bite the hand that feeds them.

Ingredients

- 2 cans of Campbell's Cream of Mushroom Soup (don't freak out!)
- (2) 7 oz cans of Ortega Mild Green Chilies (chopped, but whole is okay too)
- 2/3 cups cream (or half and half)
- 2 T butter
- 1/4 cup white wine

Cooking Steps

Put the mushroom soup, chilis, and cream in a food processor or blender and mix until smooth. Pour into a pan and heat. Add the butter and, depending on how thick or thin you like your soup, add the wine.

This recipe is from a wonderful tavern, cowboy bar and fabulous restaurant. My girlfriend got the recipe from a waitress years ago, or so legend has it. Sounds too simple? Trust me, it is delicious!

Lotsa Greens $oup (By Our Advisor, Banker, and Friend, Leonard Leo)

He's a busy guy. A modern day 'banker, baker, candlestick maker,' pulling so many strings!

Ingredients

- 1 onion, chopped
- 2 leeks, trimmed and sliced down the middle and sliced
- 3 cloves garlic
- 2 stalks celery, sliced
- Olive oil
- 3 carrots, sliced
- 1 lb. hot spicy sausage (or more if you like meaty soup)
- 1 lb. ham (packaged ham steak)
- 12 to 16 cups chicken broth
- 1 large can whole or diced tomatoes
- Greens: Lots and lots of different greens, washed and spun, including any or all of the following: kale, chard, carrot top greens, spinach, cabbage, beet greens, radish greens, kohlrabi greens, arugula, escarole. You should have at least 2 big colanders full, but more is better since it cooks down to nothing. Loosely cut the greens (especially the kale and chard since they do not break down as much).
- Salt and pepper to taste
- Parmesan Cheese

Cooking Steps

Sauté the onions, leeks, celery, and garlic in olive oil in a large pot until soft. Sauté the sausage until browned. Drain the cooked sausage on a paper towel. The spicy sausage is a must since the soup is bland without it.

Add the broth and can of tomatoes to the sautéed vegetables and bring to a boil. Add the greens (they will wilt down to nothing). Add the carrots, sausage, ham, and turn down to a simmer. Simmer on low for about an hour to an hour and a half.

This is the base but is also a good final soup so you can stop here. Or you can add more items if you like such as garbanzo beans, canned white beans, a little pasta, frozen peas, and corn if you want more of a minestrone. You can add boiled shredded chicken (if you are a serious carnivore), parsley, diced potatoes (add so the potatoes are cooked, but not mushy), diced kohlrabi, diced turnips, fresh herbs, rice, kidney beans, barley, lentils, farro…the sky's the limit. Go for it! I am not a purist! Scour your pantry or vegetable bin. Just check the cooking time (like with potatoes) with additions like rice, farro, barley etc. to make sure you add them with enough time to coordinate with the soup cooking time.

Adjust for salt and pepper and serve with parmesan cheese and crusty French bread.

We started making this soup because of the excess vegetables from our vegetable garden that seemed to go to waste.

Tomato Basil Soup (For Those Sun-Drenched Free Vacations We Love!)

Doesn't everyone get a three-month paid vacation like the Supreme Court? And as an added bonus, it's during the cruising and salmon fishing high season!

Ingredients

- 1 1/2 lbs. ripe Roma tomatoes, cut in half lengthwise
- 3 T olive oil
- 2 tsp kosher salt
- 1/2 tsp pepper
- 3 cloves garlic
- 1 onion
- 1 T butter
- 1/2 tsp crushed red pepper flakes
- 14 oz can plum tomatoes
- 1 cup fresh basil leaves, packed
- 1 1/2 tsp fresh thyme leaves
- 1 quart chicken (low salt) or vegetable broth (I use chicken)
- 1/2 cup cream

Cooking Steps

Heat the oven to 400F degrees.

Toss together the tomatoes with 1 1/2 T of the olive oil, salt, and pepper. Spread the tomatoes in one layer on a cookie sheet with the cut side up. Roast the tomatoes for 45 minutes.

In a 5-quart stockpot, sauté the onions, 1 1/2 T of olive oil, butter, and the red pepper flakes over medium heat for 10 minutes until the onions are translucent. Add the canned tomatoes, basil, thyme leaves, chicken stock, and the roasted tomatoes and any liquid on the cookie sheet. Bring to a boil and simmer for 40 minutes uncovered.

Cool a little and puree with an immersion blender or in a blender (I like the soup somewhat chunky, so I use an immersion blender. If you use a blender, pulse, and watch it carefully to keep it chunky-ish.)

Return the soup to the pot and stir in the cream. Check for seasoning. Serve hot, cold or at room temperature. I like to make it a day ahead and serve it at room temperature. I usually use a dollop of crème fraiche and some chopped chives on top when ready to serve.

Court Corruption Salad (Corrupt? Us? Nah!)

Ideology, hubris, corruption, arrogance, chutzpah, haughtiness, and a coddled egg all tossed together.

Ingredients

- 2 oz (one tin) of flat fillet anchovies in olive oil
- 2 cloves of garlic
- 1 T Dijon mustard
- 1 T Worcestershire sauce
- 1/4 cup vinegar
- 1/8 to 1/4 tsp cayenne
- Lawry's seasoning salt (several shakes)
- 1/2 lemon juiced (maybe a little more, to taste)
- 1/2 cup grated parmesan cheese
- 1 egg coddled
- 1/2 cup olive oil
- Croutons
- Romaine lettuce
- Parmesan cheese, grated

Cooking Steps

Put the full tin of anchovies with the oil (do not panic*), and the garlic into a blender or food processor. Pulse until fairly chopped. Add the mustard and mix until nearly smooth. Add the vinegar and mix. Add cayenne and Lawry's to taste. Put the egg in a cup, blend well with a fork, and microwave for 10 to 15 seconds (depending on your microwave). It should still be runny and look uncooked (not much different than when you put the egg into the microwave), but if there are a few cooked pieces they will be ground up in the mixture. Add the coddled egg, lemon juice, parmesan cheese and blend well. Slowly add the olive oil while the blender/food processor is running.

Pour the dressing over torn romaine lettuce, parmesan cheese, and croutons.

*Don't tell anyone, particularly those who tell you they hate anchovies (unless they have an allergy), they'll never know that anchovies are in the dressing, and they'll tell you they love it! Happens every time! Serves 4.

Recipe: Cheryl

Pea Salad (Settled Law Precedent Doesn't Mean Shit)

They've gotten so good at lifting their leg on legal precedent!

Ingredients

- 16 oz bag frozen petite peas
- 1/4 cup sour cream
- 1/2 cup mayonnaise
- 1 cup grated cheddar cheese
- 1/2 cup green onions
- 2 T lemon juice
- 6 slices bacon
- 1/2 cup loosely chopped dry roasted peanuts

Cooking Steps

Mix the sour cream, mayonnaise, grated cheese, green onions, and the lemon juice; you can do it ahead of time and leave in the refrigerator. When you are ready to serve, defrost the peas in a colander by running cold water over them until they are a little icy and cold (several swishes will be enough. You do not want the peas totally defrosted or mushy). Drain, mix with the premixed ingredients. Add the bacon and peanuts, toss, and serve.

Recipe: Shirley

Cherrymandering Cherry Tomato Salad (Carving Out Favorable Republican Districts)

It takes judicial teamwork to keep minorities from voting and the country permanently divided! To wit: In 2023, South Carolina's gerrymandered map was declared unconstitutional. The Supreme Court heard arguments in October 2023. Five months of inaction by the court on this redistricting case has forced a lower court to order that the state's 2024 elections be conducted with a map that includes a district it found to be racially gerrymandered. Mission Accomplished! Six-way "wink and nod"!

Ingredients

- 4 cups cherry tomatoes (a little less than 2 pints)
- 1/3 cup basil, rolled and julienned or chopped
- 1/2 thin baguette (if you can't find sourdough, a French baguette will do)
- 3/4 cup olive oil
- 1/4 cup balsamic vinegar
- 1 clove garlic, minced
- Salt and pepper to taste

Cooking Steps

Slice the half baguette (you can use more or less depending on your preference) the long ways and cut the pieces into croutons (err on the larger side). Toss the croutons with a 1/4 cup olive oil and sauté over medium heat, cooking them until they are crunchy and a golden color. Remove from heat and set aside.

Depending on the size of the cherry tomatoes, cut them in half or quarters, or if they are small, leave them whole.

Mix the remaining 1/2 cup olive oil and balsamic vinegar together and add the minced garlic clove. When you are ready to eat, mix the tomatoes, croutons, basil, dressing, and salt and pepper to taste. Serve immediately.

You can really doozie this salad up with small mozzarella balls, red bell pepper, olives, shallots, or red onion, but I don't. I like the freshness of the tomatoes and the crunch of the croutons. We grow our own cherry tomatoes and basil, and this simple salad is like a celebration of summer. Serves 4 to 6.

No One's Above the (S)Law (Except 'You Know Who')

If only that were true! Unfortunately, in America, if you have enough money, you can stall, delay, obfuscate, appeal, and suspend a trial (and then wash, rinse, and repeat with more phony baloney appeals), and inchmeal your way through the legal morass in slow motion for years if not decades. It is a sad state of affairs, but accurate; the wealthy definitely have a different legal glide path than the rest of us.

Ingredients

- Cabbage
- Mayonnaise
- Dijon mustard
- Chinese toasted sesame oil
- Cilantro
- Salt and pepper to taste
- Toasted sesame seeds

Cooking Steps

Shred half the cabbage with a knife (depending how fine you like it and adjust the amount to how many you are serving). You can do that ahead of time and keep in the refrigerator.

Mix approximately the ratio of 2/3 mayo with 1/3 Dijon mustard. Add sesame oil to taste. Try and gauge the quantities on how much cabbage to how much dressing…it will get easier after you make it a few times. The dressing will last in the refrigerator if you make it ahead or make too much.

Toss the cabbage with the dressing when you are ready to serve and mix in the chopped, stemmed cilantro (we use a lot; again, the amount depends on how much coleslaw you are making and how much you like cilantro) and sprinkle with toasted sesame seeds. Add salt and pepper to taste.

Recipe: Shirley

Cold Chinese Salad (Minorities, Forget About Affirmative Action)

In June 2023, the court's 6-3 ruling prohibited all colleges in the country from using race as a consideration in admissions. Legacy admissions go to the front of the line! Minorities to the back. Surprised?

This is a good cold noodle, mix and match, kitchen sink kind of salad. It is especially good on a hot day, and much easier than it looks at first glance.

<u>Ingredients</u>

- Noodles: We use packaged wheat or rice noodles. Options include Ramen, Soba, Somen, Vermicelli, Udon; any type will work. I usually use Ramen, Somen, or Udon, about 8 to 10 oz. Available in the Chinese section of the market. Use package directions to cook the noodles.
- Vegetables (raw): Snap peas (string and slice in thin strips) Napa cabbage, a half of a large head cut in half lengthwise. Lay half flat and thinly slice in half-moons. (The Napa cabbage is key in this salad. Do not skip.) Green onions sliced or cut on the diagonal or just sliced if you are lazy like I am. Peel one kohlrabi and slice into matchsticks).
- Protein Options: Chicken (rotisserie is a good option and easy; remove the meat from the bones), shrimp, or leftovers steak or pork… or a

combination. (Amount depends on your taste: We are carnivores!)

- Toppings: Sliced basil, cilantro, chopped chives or green onions, chopped dry roasted peanuts, sesame seeds, jalapeños. (My daughter is a fire eater so I put the jalapeño on the side so she can add more as a topping for the salad.)
- Dressing: 3/4 cup smooth peanut butter, 3 T rice vinegar, 3 T soy sauce, 3 T sesame oil, Chinese fish sauce to taste, hot chili oil or sriracha (a few squeezes if you like spicy), fresh ginger grated, several tablespoons of Ginger Honey Concentrate to taste (buy online, see note), lime juice, and possibly a drop of maple syrup or sugar if you can't find ginger tea, this is a guide. Use any of the listed items or omit some. It is different every time I make it but always good. You may need more sesame oil and soy, or not. The heat depends on how your family likes it. Just mix and taste until you like it.

Cooking Steps

Cook the noodles according to package directions, drain and run under cold water to stop the cooking. Toss with sesame oil (unlike the judges on *Chopped*, we love sesame oil and use it generously) so they won't clump together and dry out. You can make it ahead and refrigerate.

Chop the vegetable into bite-size pieces. You can do this ahead of time too. I use rotisserie chicken; the amount depends on how much you want and/or how many people you are serving. Use the leftover chicken for sandwiches or dinner depending how much you have left. Sometimes I add some shrimp too, but this is optional.

Mix the above with the noodles and add the basil, cilantro, green onions, and peanuts (lots), and toss with the dressing and serve. It's okay the next day, especially if you don't mix the peanuts into the noodles when you toss. I never worry about it because we always finish the salad, but it's still good for lunch if you have any left. Sometimes I add some shrimp, too, but this is optional.

Note: I use Han Cha Kan Ginger Honey Concentrate. It's also known as Ginger Tea. Sometimes you can find it in Asian markets. Put a spoonful into your tea. Delicious. Benefits of Ginger tea? There are numerous benefits that come from drinking ginger tea including nausea relief, relief from coughs, supporting heart health, weight management and weight loss. Who knew?

Wild Rice Salad (Girls Go Wild When You Take Away Their Reproductive Rights)

They have no idea just how wild. But they will. Soon.

Ingredients

- 1 cup wild rice
- 1 1/4 cups chicken broth
- 1 clove garlic
- 1 bunch scallions, finely chopped
- 2 T butter
- 1 cup (about 1/4 lb.) chopped mushrooms (large chop)
- 3 strips lean bacon, sliced, and fried crisp
- 1/2 cup chopped green olives with pimento
- 1/3 cup olive oil
- 3 T lemon juice
- 1 T fresh tarragon, chopped or 1 tsp dried tarragon
- 1/2 tsp dried marjoram
- 1 T capers, drained
- 1/2 packed Italian parsley, chopped
- Salt and pepper to taste

Cooking Steps

Soak the wild rice in water overnight. Rinse the rice and then simmer in chicken broth with the garlic, in a covered pan.

Cook until the liquid is absorbed, about 25 to 30 minutes. The wild rice should be fluffy. Discard the garlic.

Melt the butter in a medium-sized pan over high heat and toss the mushrooms briefly. Cool, drain liquid, then mix rice with the other ingredients and toss well, seasoning with salt and pepper.

Chill, preferably for 24 hours. Toss once more, rechecking for salt since the wild rice can absorb it, and serve the salad cold. Perfect for a picnic, tailgate, or a BBQ side dish. Dish up on a plate, or serve on butter leaf lettuce, spooning the wild rice salad on the lettuce leaf and rolling it up like a sandwich. If you want a heartier salad for dinner on a warm night, add 1 cup cooked large diced cold chicken or ham. Serves 6 to 8.

Undermining the Rule of Law Lasagna (Our Favorite Dish)

After years of practice, they've become experts at it!

Look no further, I have done the leg work, this is the best lasagna recipe ... ever! Just ask my friend Lise.

Ingredients

Meat Sauce

- 1/2 lb. lasagna noodles (oven-ready lasagna noodles work too, and are much easier)
- 1 lb. ground beef
- 1/2 chopped onion
- 3 cloves garlic, minced
- 1 T olive oil
- 3 lbs. tomatoes (6 to 7 large) peeled, seeded, and chopped, (or canned tomatoes, drained)
- 1 1/2 tsp seasoned salt
- 2 T chopped parsley (or 1 tsp dried)
- 2 T chopped fresh basil (or 1 tsp dried)
- 1/2 tsp oregano
- 1/4 tsp ground pepper

Cooking Steps

If you are using standard noodles, cook in boiling salted water until 'al dente'. Drain and keep them in cold water until ready to use.

Sauté ground beef, onion, and garlic in olive oil until the meat is no longer pink. Add remaining ingredients and cook at a fast simmer until the sauce is quite thick (about 30 to 40 minutes). Drain the fat.

Bechamel
- 1/2 cup butter
- 4 T flour
- 1 cup milk
- 1 cup chicken broth
- 1/8 tsp salt

Melt butter, add flour, and cook, stirring with a whisk, for one minute.

Slowly add milk and chicken broth and bring to a boil, still using a whisk. Add salt.

Ricotta Filling
- 1 egg
- 1/2 lb. ricotta cheese
- 1/4 cup Parmesan cheese
- 1/8 t nutmeg
- 1/2 t salt

Beat egg in a bowl. Add remaining ingredients and stir well with a fork.

Cheeses
- 1 1/2 grated Parmesan cheese
- 4 oz mozzarella cheese, sliced
- 4 oz teleme cheese (you can substitute bergamino cheese if you can't find teleme. If you are really in a pinch, crescenza or brie with the rind removed will work too)
- Butter

Heat the oven to 400F degrees.

Prepare all the above ingredients first. In the following order, layer in a lightly greased 13 x 9 (or two 9 x 9 pans) baking dish: a little (scant amount) meat sauce, half of the noodles (if you are using the oven ready just place on the sauce etc.), half of the remaining meat sauce, 1/2 cup bechamel, 1/2 cup parmesan cheese, half of the mozzarella, teleme, and ricotta (note: I break the cheese slices into little pieces and dot over the pan).

Add the remaining noodles and meat sauce, 1/2 cup bechamel, 1/2 cup parmesan cheese, half of the mozzarella, teleme, and ricotta; and remaining bechamel, and parmesan cheeses. Dot with butter. At this point, the dish may be covered and refrigerated or frozen.

From room temperature, bake uncovered, for 40 to 45 minutes or more, until a little bubbly. This dish freezes very well. Since there are a lot of steps, I always make at least two and have several in my freezer. Serves 12 as a pasta or 8 as an entrée.

Recipe: Private Collection

Carbonara (For 'Good Guys With a Gun,' Except at the Supreme Court)

Luckily for them they don't have to deal with the everyday threats like the rest of us… work, school, movies, malls, church, and Super Bowl parades, to name a few! This is a 'supreme' pasta that has a place in the hallowed halls of the court!

Ingredients

- 1 1/2 to 2 lbs. spaghetti
- 1 1/4 lbs. Italian sausage. (I use half mild, with fennel, and half hot. If you end up with a little extra sausage don't worry!)
- 1 lb. domestic prosciutto, sliced 1/4-inch thick
- 8 T butter
- 3 eggs whisked
- 1/2 cup chopped parsley
- 1 cup cream (more or less)
- Fresh grated parmesan cheese to taste

Cooking Steps

Cut the prosciutto into 1/4-inch cubes. Remove the casings from the sausage and cook in 2 T of butter. When the sausage is partially cooked (about 5 min.), add 1/2 the prosciutto to the pan and complete cooking the sausage. Remove from the heat and drain off the grease. Then add the remaining uncooked 1/2 of the prosciutto to the pan, without cooking. This can be done ahead of assembling the carbonara.

About 10 minutes before you are ready to serve the carbonara, cook the spaghetti. Once done, remove a cup of the pasta water and set aside. Drain the spaghetti and toss with 6 T of butter.

Have all the other ingredients prepared and ready to assemble. Take the drained spaghetti tossed with butter (let the noodles cool a couple of minutes) and add the cream, and then carefully add the eggs a little at a time to make sure you don't scramble the eggs. Add the sausage, prosciutto, parmesan cheese, and parsley.

This is a guideline. If the pasta is too dry, add more cream, or a little pasta water, and extra parmesan cheese until the carbonara is well mixed, hot, and creamy. I have been known to begin the mixing of the ingredients with gloves on my hands (most of the time), and then as the carbonara is getting warmer, I use two large spoons or tongs trying to keep the noodles from breaking too much. Okay, I acknowledge this is a totally fattening dish, so we only serve it on Christmas Eve…a tradition for over 40 years! It sounds complicated, but I've assembled this after several egg nogs; it is not that hard, just watch the eggs! Serves 6 to 8.

Gourmet Mac and Cheese (Thomas' Walmart Parking Lot Nostalgia Delight!)

Just in case your RV is parked in front of your billionaire handler's home.

Ingredients

- 1 1/2 cups coarse fresh breadcrumbs (preferably from a rustic, sourdough-style loaf)
- 2 oz extra-sharp cheddar, coarsely grated
- 3 T grated Parmigiano-Reggiano
- 2 T chopped flat-leaf parsley
- 2 T unsalted butter, melted
- 3 T unsalted butter
- 3 T all-purpose flour
- 2 cups whole milk
- 1/2 cup heavy cream
- 2 tsp dry mustard
- 2 tsp Worcestershire sauce
- 12 oz extra-sharp cheddar (white, yellow, or a mix of both), coarsely grated
- 1/3 cup grated Parmigiano-Reggiano
- 3/4 tsp salt
- 1/2 tsp pepper
- 1/2 lb. curly macaroni, such as cavatappi, chifferi, fusilli or good old elbow
- 2 1/2-quart shallow baking dish

Cooking Steps

Heat oven to 400°F degrees with a rack in the middle of the oven.

Toast breadcrumbs on a rimmed baking sheet until pale golden, about 5 minutes. When cool, toss crumbs with cheese, parsley, and melted butter with a fork until butter is evenly incorporated. Leave the oven on.

Melt butter in a medium-heavy saucepan over medium-low heat and whisk In the flour. Cook roux, whisking, 3 minutes, then whisk in the milk. Bring the sauce to a boil, whisking constantly, then simmer, whisking occasionally, for 3 minutes. Whisk in the cream, mustard, Worcestershire, cheeses, 3/4 tsp salt, and 1/2 tsp pepper until smooth and remove from the heat. Cover the surface of the sauce with wax paper or parchment. Cook the macaroni in a pot of well-salted boiling water until al dente. Drain in a colander. Transfer to a bowl and stir in sauce. Spread the macaroni mixture evenly in a 2 to 2 1/2-quart shallow baking dish.

Sprinkle the bread crumb topping evenly over macaroni. Bake until golden and bubbling, 20 to 25 minutes. Serves 6 to 8.

Recipe: *Gourmet Magazine*

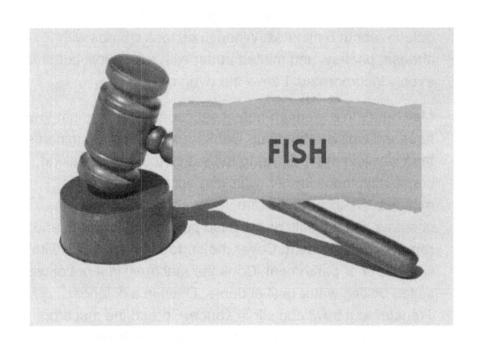

Charlottesville Rally Shrimp and Grits (For the "Very Good People on Both Sides")

The very good people were only on one side. Just saying…

Ingredients

- 1 lb. jumbo raw shrimp, peeled, and deveined; reserve the shrimp peels
- 2 cups chicken broth
- 4 slices bacon, cut into strips crosswise
- 1 bunch green onions, sliced
- 1 green bell pepper, diced
- 2 garlic cloves
- 1/2 lb. smoked Andouille sausage, sliced in 1/2-inch slices
- 2 cups chicken broth
- 2 tsp smoked paprika
- 2 tsp garlic powder
- 1 tsp oregano
- 1 tsp dried thyme
- 1/2 tsp cayenne (3/4 tsp if you like your food spicier)
- 1/2 tsp dried basil
- 1/2 tsp dried marjoram
- 1/4 tsp fennel pollen
- 1 tsp salt
- 1 tsp pepper
- 3 T flour

- 1 cup drained canned tomatoes
- 1 dash Tabasco (optional)

Cooking Steps

Cook the bacon until crispy and remove from the pan. Drain the bacon grease leaving approximately 2 T in the pan.

Shrimp stock: Put the shells in the chicken stock and boil for 5 minutes, drain the shells and reserve the stock. Alternately, you can cook the unpeeled shrimp in the chicken stock just until they are done. Drain and reserve the stock, peel the shrimp, and add it just before serving.

Mix bacon grease, green onions, bell pepper, and garlic and cook over medium heat until softened, about 5 minutes. Add the sliced sausage and cook until browned. Add the herbs and cook, stirring, for several minutes. Add the flour and cook, stirring the mixture until incorporated and the flour is heated. Add the shrimp stock in increments until you have creamy textured sauce. If you need more liquid, add more chicken broth and cook over high heat for 7 to 10 minutes. Add the shrimp and cook until they are pink.

Grits
- 1 cup stone ground grits (not fast cooking)
- 3 cups milk (non-fat or 2% is okay)
- 1 cup chicken stock
- 1/4 cup butter
- 1/2 tsp salt
- 1/2 tsp pepper
- 1 cup shredded sharp cheddar cheese

In a large saucepan, bring broth, milk, butter, salt, and pepper to a boil. Slowly stir in the grits and whisk until mixed. Reduce heat. Cover and simmer for 15 to 20 minutes stirring occasionally, until thickened. Stir in the cheese until melted. Take off the heat and serve. If you need to reheat, add a splash of chicken broth, and reheat over low heat in a small saucepan stirring frequently to prevent sticking.

Put the grits in a bowl and spoon the shrimp and sauce over the grits. Sprinkle the cooked bacon over the shrimp. Serves 4.

Shrimp Fajitas with Arrogant Bastard Ale (Inspired by Neil Gorsuch)

What more is there to say?

Ingredients

- 1 T olive oil
- 2 cups sliced bell peppers red, orange, yellow, or a combination
- 1 onion, thinly sliced
- 1 tsp chili powder
- 1 tsp chipotle powder
- 1/2 tsp ground cumin
- 1/4 tsp garlic powder
- 1/4 tsp onion powder
- 1/2 tsp smoked paprika
- 4 T chopped cilantro
- 1 lb. large shrimp, peeled and deveined
- 1/3 cup Arrogant Bastard Ale (available in most large liquor stores and outlets. If you can't find Arrogant Bastard Ale, substitute any ale)
- Flour tortillas (or if you can find 1/2 flour and 1/2 corn tortillas even better!)
- Salt and pepper to taste

Cooking Steps

Heat the oil in a large pan over high heat. Add the peppers and onion to the pan and cook, stirring occasionally, until vegetables are tender and charred on the edges. Season the vegetables with salt and pepper. Set aside.

In a small bowl, mix the chili powder, chipotle powder, cumin, garlic powder, onion powder, smoked paprika, and salt and pepper to taste.

Add the shrimp to the pan and sprinkle the seasoning blend over the shrimp. Stir to combine. Add the 1/3 cup of Arrogant Ale and cook for 4 to 5 minutes or until shrimp are done and the ale is evaporated.

Add the vegetables and sprinkle the cilantro over the top and serve with flour tortillas, toppings, and jalapeño dressing on the side, and have everyone assemble their own fajitas.

Fajita toppings
   • Grated cheese
   • Lime wedges
   • Chopped cilantro
   • Salsa

Jalapeño Dressing (This is a must for the fajitas!)
   • 1 cup sour cream (you can substitute plain yogurt)
   • 1/2 cup cilantro
   • 1 jalapeño, seeded and cut into pieces
   • 2 tsp lime juice
   • 1 tsp salt

- 1/4 cup onion, cut into pieces
- 2 cloves garlic
- 1 tsp dry ranch dressing

Put all ingredients in a blender and mix until smooth. Serves 4 to 6.

Truffled Lobster Risotto (Loan Forgiveness for Me, but Not for Thee)

The bigshot PPP borrowers were forgiven, but thanks to the Supreme Court, students are still on the hook!

Ingredients

- 1 1/2 lb. uncooked lobster tails
- 5 1/4 cups low salt chicken broth
- 4 1/2 T truffle oil
- 1/3 cup finely chopped onions
- 1 1/2 cups arborio rice
- 1/3 cup brandy
- 1/2 cup cream

Cooking Steps

Heat the oven to 425F degrees.

Cook lobster tails in a large pot of simmering salted water until cooked through. (I put the lobster tails on a vegetable steamer in a pot of boiling water to steam the lobsters). Transfer to a bowl of cold water to cool. Drain the lobster, remove the meat from the shells and cut the meat into 1/2-inch pieces.

Break shells into large pieces. Place on a baking sheet; bake for 15 minutes. Blend the shells with 1 1/2 cups of the chicken broth in a blender until finely chopped. Strain through a fine sieve. Reserve lobster broth, discard the shells. Alternately, you can boil the chicken broth and cook the shells in the broth for 5 minutes. Cool and strain.

Bring the remaining 3 3/4 cups of chicken broth to a simmer. Keep hot. Heat 1 1/2 T truffle oil in a heavy large pan over medium heat. Add onions and sauté for 2 minutes. Add the rice and stir for 2 minutes. Add brandy and reduce the heat to medium-low and simmer until the brandy is absorbed, stirring constantly, about 2 minutes. Add lobster broth and 3/4 cup of the chicken broth and simmer until the rice is just tender and creamy. Add remaining broth 1/4 cup at a time as needed and stir often, about 20 minutes.

Add lobster and cream and stir until heated through. Remove from heat stir in 3 T truffle oil and chives. Season with salt and white pepper. Serves 4.

King Salmon With Horseradish and Caper Sauce (Served on Private Jets)

When you sneak home with illicit spoils, you need a tasty recipe!!

Ingredients

- 2 lbs. boneless, skinless salmon fillets
- 1/2 cup sour cream
- 2 1/2 T prepared horseradish
- 1 T chopped capers
- 2 T chopped green onions
- 1 T chopped tarragon
- 1/8 tsp paprika
- 1/4 lemon, juiced
- 1/2 tsp salt plus salt for sprinkling on the fish

Cooking Steps

Heat the oven to 400F degrees.

Combine sour cream, horseradish, capers, green onions, tarragon, paprika, and lemon juice.

Sprinkle the salmon with salt and brush the fish with about 1/4 cup, or less, of the sauce and bake for approximately 15 to 20 minutes, depending on the thickness of the salmon, or until the fish flakes with a fork.

Serve the remaining sauce with the cooked fish.

Optional: Lightly sprinkle the fish with Panko before baking to add a little "crunch." This sauce is good on flounder, halibut, cod, or any mild firm fish. Serves 4 to 6.

Senator Kerr's Chinese Houseboy's Beef Tenderloin (Ah, the Good Ol' Days)

It always helps to have a houseboy to cook and serve! It's an old recipe. Senator Kerr was in the Senate from 1948 to 1963. This is so much better than you would imagine given the ingredients are not sexy.

My girlfriend is from Oklahoma, and she gave me this recipe. We always use it on a big, fabulous hunk of beef tenderloin or filet strip, etc.

Ingredients

- 1 1/2 cups salad oil (not olive, more like canola)
- 3/4 cups soy sauce
- 1/4 cup Worcestershire sauce
- 2 T dry mustard
- 2 1/2 tsp salt
- 1 T coarse ground pepper
- 1/2 cup wine vinegar
- 1 1/2 tsp dried parsley
- 2 crushed garlic cloves
- 1/2 cup fresh lemon juice

Cooking Steps

Mix all the ingredients in a bowl. Put the meat in a plastic food storage bag and marinate the meat for at least a couple of hours.

Heat the oven to 425F degrees.

Drain the meat, then put it in a pan and cook until a meat thermometer reads about 125F degrees (check periodically). Take out of the oven, cover the meat, and let sit for 10 to15 minutes before carving/serving.

Brett's Beer Chili ("So Sue Me, I Like Beer!")

'So, sue me, I like beer,' Supreme Court nominee Brett Kavanaugh announced to national TV audiences!

Ingredients

- 2 T olive oil
- 2 lbs. lean ground beef (chili grind or regular hamburger)
- 3/4 lb. top sirloin (cut in bite-size pieces)
- 2 medium onions, chopped
- 2 garlic cloves, finely chopped
- 28 oz can whole tomatoes
- 12 oz beer (not lite)
- 5 T chili powder
- 2 jalapeños, seeded and chopped (1 if you are a wimp)
- 1 T cumin
- 1 tsp sugar (optional)
- Cooked rice

Cooking Steps

Toppings: cheddar cheese, red onion, chopped, sour cream, cilantro, and chopped avocado.

Heat oil in 6-quart pan. Add the beef and brown, draining fat if needed. Add the onion and garlic, and sauté until soft. Stir in the next seven ingredients and bring to a boil, reduce heat to medium low, and simmer uncovered for about 1 hour. Taste and season with salt and pepper.

There are lots of variations available. Sometimes, I substitute one of the T of chili powder with chipotle or ancho chili powder. You can use a couple of canned chipotle chilies (seeded) if you like the smoky flavor and cut out one of the jalapeños, or not. You can add a can or a couple of cans of pinto or kidney beans if you like beans.

I always double the recipe so I can freeze some for a night when I want something fast and easy. Serve over rice with the toppings listed above.

Cola Can Burgers (Only Those 'Over the Hill' Will Get It)

If you 'young'uns' are confused, look up Anita Hill! These burgers are especially delicious if you are BBQing in the Walmart parking lot while parked in your free RV.

Ingredients

- 1 1/2 lbs. hamburger
- 1 egg, lightly beaten
- 1/2 cup cola
- 1/2 cup saltine crackers, crushed
- 6 T Catalina Dressing
- 2 T parmesan cheese
- 1/2 tsp salt
- 1/2 tsp pepper
- 6 or 8 Brioche buns (depends on your burger size)

Cooking Steps

Combine the beef, egg, 1/4 cup cola, crackers, 2 T Catalina dressing, cheese, and salt, and mix well. Shape 6 to 8 patties, depending on the size you want. In a bowl, combine the remaining cola and dressing.

Grill patties on a BBQ for 3 minutes a side. Brush on the remaining cola mixture while cooking. Or cook uncovered in a frying pan until juices run clear, basting and turning, as needed.

Serve on buns. Add the usual condiments: cheese, tomatoes, pickles, lettuce, onion etc. For the adventurous, add a little cola and Catalina to the mayo, and spread on buns. You can also substitute Dr. Pepper for the cola if you prefer.

Note: These burgers can stick to the grill and are fairly fragile. Be sure your grill grates are greased and that your grill is hot before adding the burgers. Do not flip them a ton of times. Serves 6 to 8.

Chicken and Prunes (Thanks, Mitch, for Stealing Obama's Supreme Court Seat!)

Classic Republican dick move.

Here's a great winter dinner by the fire, after you've packed your bags in disgust and moved off the grid.

Ingredients

- 4 whole chicken legs (thigh and drumsticks not separated)
- 1/2 cup olive oil
- 1 1/2 cups red wine
- 1 1/2 cups dry marsala
- 1 tsp dried thyme
- 1 cup dried prunes (pitted)
- 4 cloves garlic, crushed
- Salt and pepper

Cooking Steps

Marinate the chicken in 6 T olive oil, red wine, half the marsala, thyme, and prunes until the prunes are softish, about 2 hours. Drain and save the marinade and prunes.

Heat the remaining olive oil in a large pan or casserole and sauté the garlic and chicken until the chicken is browned all over.

Pour the remaining marsala over the chicken and continue until the marsala has reduced by 2/3. Then add the reserved marinade with the prunes into the pan with the chicken. Season with salt and pepper, cover, reduce the heat, and simmer very gently for 1 1/2 to 2 hours. Take the lid off toward the end, if necessary, to reduce the liquid to a rich sauce. Serve over noodles or rice. Serves 4.

Chicken and Sausage Stew With Mushrooms (By Chief Chicken, John Roberts)

You can thank him – and Thomas, Kavanaugh, and Coney Barrett for George W. Bush and the Iraq War. Damn those 'hanging chads.'

Ingredients

- 1/2 cup of dried porcini mushrooms
- 3/4 cup boiling water
- 2 T olive oil
- 2 cups sliced button mushrooms
- 2 cups sliced shiitake mushrooms (stems removed)
- 1 1/2 lbs. skinless, boneless, chicken breast halves or thighs cut into 1-inch (or a tad bigger) pieces
- 1/2 lbs. sweet Italian sausage
- 1/4 lbs. spicy sausage (you can use Italian or Chicken sausage)
- 2 T butter
- 1 medium onion, chopped
- 3 large cloves garlic, minced
- 3 T flour
- 14 1/2 oz (full can) of chicken stock or broth
- 1 1/2 tsp snipped fresh rosemary or 1/2 tsp dried rosemary, crushed
- 1 tsp snipped fresh thyme, or 1/2 tsp dried thyme, crushed
- 14 1/2 oz can diced and drained tomatoes

Cooking Steps

Place dried porcini mushrooms in a small bowl and add boiling water. Let stand for 30 minutes or until the mushrooms are softened. Drain the mushrooms, reserving the liquid. Cut up any large pieces of mushrooms. Set mushrooms and reserved liquid aside.

Heat 1 T oil in a skillet over medium heat. Add the button and shiitake mushrooms. Cook and stir for 3 minutes or until the mushrooms are tender. Remove from heat and stir in the porcini mushrooms. Set it aside.

In a heavy 4-quart Dutch oven, heat remaining 1 T olive oil over medium heat. Season chicken pieces with salt and pepper. Brown the chicken in two batches. Remove the chicken from the pan. Add the sausage pieces to the pan and brown. Remove the sausage from the pan. Drain off the fat, leaving brown bits in the pan. Return the pan to medium heat. Add butter, onion, and garlic. Cook and stir for 3 to 5 minutes or until the onion is softened.

Sprinkle the flour over the onion mixture. Cook and stir constantly for 5 minutes or until the flour is browned. Add chicken stock, the reserved mushroom liquid, the drained tomatoes, rosemary, and thyme. Cook and stir over medium heat until thickened and bubbly. Add the mushroom mixture and browned chicken and sausage. Stir to coat with sauce. Reduce heat and simmer, covered, for 30 minutes or until the chicken and the sausage is done, stirring once. Serve over rice. Consider making a double batch, as it freezes beautifully. Serves 6 to 8.

Mumbo Jumbo Gumbo (a.k.a. The Major Questions Doctrine)

The major questions doctrine is a new word salad doctrine the court made up to outwit us, again.

Ingredients

- 1 cup all-purpose flour
- 2/3 cup vegetable oil
- 1 bunch celery, diced
- 2 green bell pepper, diced
- 2 large yellow onion, diced
- 1 bunch green onion, chopped
- 3 cloves garlic
- 2 bay leaves
- 1 tsp cayenne
- 1 tsp paprika
- 1 tsp black pepper
- 3/4 tsp white pepper
- 1 tsp oregano
- 2 tsp dried thyme
- 1 tsp file (optional)
- 6 to 8 cups chicken broth
- 2 lbs. or about 3 boneless, skinless chicken breasts or a rotisserie chicken
- 1 lb. large shrimp, peeled and deveined
- 12 oz andouille sausage, sliced in 1/2-inch rounds (use kielbasa if you cannot find andouille)
- Rice for serving

Cooking Steps

It is best to have all the ingredients prepped and ready to go before you assemble the gumbo. Chop green onions, onion, celery, and bell pepper and set aside. Cut the chicken into 1-inch pieces and brown. Remove from the pan and set aside. If you are using a rotisserie chicken (easier), remove the meat from the bones. Brown the sliced andouille sausage for about 5 minutes, flipping to brown both sides.

Peel and devein the shrimp and set aside. Take the shrimp shells and simmer in 6 cups of the chicken broth and boil the shrimp shells for 2 to 3 minutes and remove from the heat. Cool and strain out the shells. Set the broth aside.

To make roux, heat the oil in a large heavy soup pot or pan on medium heat until shimmery, about 2 minutes. Add the flour, whisking until blended. Continue whisking constantly for 25 to 45 minutes until it is the color you want; anywhere from caramel, to peanut butter color, to melted dark chocolate color. I prefer to cook the roux for about 25 minutes, when it looks like peanut butter. As a rule of thumb, the darker the roux the thicker the Gumbo. Regardless of the color, do not let it burn!

When the roux is your desired color, add the cut vegetables and cook until they are softened, about 6 to 8 minutes, stirring often. Add garlic and cook for another minute.

Add the broth to the roux and vegetables, then add the chicken, sliced cooked sausage, bay leaf, and seasonings, and boil for about 8 to 10 minutes. Turn the heat down and simmer for about 40 minutes uncovered. When you are ready to eat, add the shrimp and cook until it is no longer pink, about 3 to 4 minutes.

If the gumbo is too thick, add more broth. Serve on white rice. Serves 6 to 8.

This dish is best made at least a day before you want to serve it. It freezes beautifully.

The main difference between gumbo and jambalaya is the use of rice. Gumbo is more soup or stew like, tomato-free, and served over rice. Jambalaya has tomatoes and is made with rice cooked into the dish and is thicker.

Irish Stew With Guinness (Let's Go, Brandon!)

Would you expect less from this in-the-bag, right-wing court?

Ingredients

- 2 1/2 lbs. beef brisket or stew meat, cut into 1 1/2-inch pieces.
- Salt and pepper
- 2 T olive oil
- 2 T butter
- 3 strips bacon (cut into strips crosswise)
- 2 onions, chopped
- 1 leek, coarsely chopped
- 2 celery stalks, cut in 1-inch pieces
- 2 cloves garlic
- 3 T flour
- 4 T tomato paste
- 3 cups Guinness
- 2 cup beef broth
- 2 bay leaves
- 4 sprigs fresh thyme (1 1/2 tsp dried thyme)
- 1/4 cup chopped Italian parsley
- 3 carrots, cut into 1/2-inch slices
- 2 medium or 1 large potato, peeled and cut into bite-sized pieces
- 10 mushrooms, halved or quartered, depending on the size

Cooking Steps

Heat the oven to 350F degrees.

Salt and pepper the meat, and brown in batches in olive oil and butter until all sides are browned. (Add more olive oil and butter if needed while cooking the meat). Remove to a plate.

Cook the bacon, onions, leeks, celery, and garlic in the same pan, stirring frequently, until softened, about 10 minutes. Add flour and tomato paste and cook for 2 minutes. Add the bay leaves, thyme, Italian parsley, and browned beef.

Cover the meat with Guinness and beef broth and bake in the oven for 2 hours. Remove from the oven.

If you are serving the stew the same day you make it, stir in the carrots, mushrooms, and potatoes, and return to the oven for 1 hour more. If you are making the stew ahead of when you are serving it (which makes it better), remove the stew from the oven after 2 hours, cool and refrigerate. When you are ready to serve, warm the stew on the stove and add the carrots, mushrooms, and potatoes, and cook in a preheated 350F degree oven for 1 hour.

Once the stew is cooked and out of the oven, add butter and flour mixture using the formula of 1 T flour and 1 T butter mixed. (I may add this flour/butter ratio several times, depending on the amount of liquid there is.) This stew should be a little thicker than a normal stew. Serves 6.

Sir Matthew Hale's Lamb Shanks (From Alito's Favorite Century, the 17th)

Alito invokes Hale's "eminent common law authorities" to show how abortion is not a right, but a criminal act. Seriously. So just grab a big bone and gnaw on it, 17th-century style!

Ingredients

- 4 meaty lamb shanks (best if they are cracked…ask the butcher, but not necessary a deal breaker)
- Flour
- 1 T sugar
- Olive oil
- Dry vermouth or white wine
- 2 cloves garlic, minced
- 1 onion, chopped
- Beef stock
- Salt and pepper
- Parsley
- 1 lemon, zested
- 1 bay leaf
- 1 T thyme (or more)
- (1 or 2) 15 oz cans diced tomatoes, drained well
- 5 carrots (more or less), sliced thick
- 1 can cannellini white beans

Cooking Steps

Lightly toss the shanks in flour, and brown them in olive oil in a large pan. Sprinkle the sugar over the meat once it is browning and cook 3 to 4 more minutes until the sugar has caramelized. It should have a nice amber color. Remove the meat to a plate and deglaze the pan with the vermouth or white wine (a couple of glugs). Add the onions and garlic and cook until softened.

Add the meat back into the pan, covering the shanks with beef stock but not completely covering the meat (depending on pan size). Add the tomatoes, salt and pepper, parsley, bay leaf, thyme, and lemon zest. Bring to a boil and turn down to a simmer. Cook for about 2 hours and turn the meat halfway through. If it is cooking down too much, add more broth.

After 2 hours, add the drained beans and carrots, and cook until the carrots are tender. Serve over rice.

I know it is blasphemous, but I like risotto cooked like regular rice (2 parts water to 1 part rice) for serving with the lamb shanks. Keep an eye on it to be sure there is enough water. Somehow the larger grain of risotto seems to go better with the shanks. Cooking risotto that way can make a mess, so use a larger pan, so it does not spit and drip all over the stove. Serves 4.

Amy's 'Man-Pleasing Chicken' (The Obedient Wife's Go-To Dinner!)

The Handmaidens may say, "Blessed be the fruit...," but we'd rather bless this simple but delicious chicken recipe!

Ingredients

- 1 lb. boneless, skinless chicken thighs
- 1/2 cup Dijon mustard
- 1/4 cup maple syrup
- 1 T rice wine vinegar
- Salt and pepper
- Chopped rosemary

Cooking Steps

Heat the oven to 450F degrees.

Mix the Dijon mustard, maple syrup, and rice wine vinegar together.

Sprinkle the chicken with salt and pepper and place it in an ovenproof baking dish. Pour the mustard mixture over the thighs, turning them in the mixture so they are fully coated.

Bake for 40 minutes or until the meat is cooked. Halfway through, baste the chicken with the sauce. Let the chicken rest for 5 minutes before serving. Then sprinkle with fresh rosemary. Serves 4.

Kavanaugh's Michelada Flank Steak (With Brett's Favorite Ingredient - Lager!)

If you're man enough, drink the leftover marinade, like Brett.

Ingredients

- 2 jalapeños, cut lengthwise into half-moons and seeded
- 4 cloves garlic, chopped
- 1 T honey
- 2 T fresh lime juice
- 10 sprigs cilantro (small handful)
- 1 tsp salt
- 1 tsp black pepper
- 1 tsp Tajin or hot sauce
- 1 T Worcestershire sauce
- (1) 12 oz bottle Mexican lager
- 1 to 2 lbs. flank steak

Cooking Steps

Mix all the ingredients together and put the flank steak and the marinade in a large sealable bag and marinate for 4 to 24 hours in the refrigerator.

Remove the flank steak from the refrigerator and drain the marinade off the meat. Grill until your desired doneness. Cut across the grain. Serve with Creamy Cilantro Sauce or

Jalapeño Dressing (see **Shrimp Fajitas with Arrogant Bastard Ale**) or both!

Creamy Cilantro Sauce
- 3/4 cup sour cream
- 3/4 cup cilantro leaves
- 2 cloves garlic, diced
- 1 1/2 to 2 jalapeño or poblano chilies, seeded (depending on your spice tolerance)
- 1/2 cup green onion, loosely chopped
- 2 T lime juice
- 1/2 t salt

Mix in a food processor or blender.

Noodles Marmaduke (Because Ethics Codes are for Peasants!)

This is a poor man's stroganoff, but it is easy, fast, and the perfect comfort food for the lower court schlubs who are forced to follow an ethics code.

Ingredients

- 1 lb. lean hamburger meat
- 1 onion, sliced in half and then half moons
- 1/4 cup butter
- Mushrooms, sliced (you can use as many as you like)
- 1 lemon, juiced
- Red wine (a good glug or two)
- 16 oz egg noodles or the noodles of your choice
- 22 oz beef broth
- 1 pint of sour cream

Cooking Steps

Sauté the onions and mushrooms in the butter and then add the hamburger and cook until browned. Add the wine and lemon juice. Put the noodles on top of the meat and add the broth. The recipe may need a little water if it seems too dry. When the noodles are cooked, add the sour cream and heat through. Serve immediately. Serves 4.

Recipe: *The Bryan Ohio 3 Martini Cookbook.* Recipes that you can make after you've had three martinis.

LGBTQueso and Meat Stuffed Chili Rellenos (Blackened, Just Like Our Hearts)

Their mission? Alito and his legal doppelganger, Thomas, have made a pinky-promise to overturn the Obergefell decision which requires states to allow same-sex marriages. And here's how it can work: On 2/20/24, Alito released a missive criticizing same-sex marriage, and on 2/21/24, Tennessee Governor Bill Lee signed a bill that allows public officials to refuse to perform same-sex marriages due to "conscience or religious beliefs," thereby violating the Obergefell decision. Voila, the Obergefell decision is now primed for the Supreme Court to review. What a lucky coincidence!

Ingredients

- 4 poblano chilies
- 1 lb. lean hamburger
- 1 can black beans
- 1 corn off the cob or a can of corn
- Cumin to taste
- Ancho chili powder to taste
- 1 can Hatch or fresh jalapeño chili
- Cilantro (mix in with meat mixture and some to sprinkle on top after it is baked)
- 1 jar Herdez green salsa (I use about half of the jar)

- Green onions (for mixture and to sprinkle on top after it is baked)
- Pepper jack cheese to taste
- 1 cup cooked rice
- Cherry tomatoes

Cooking Steps

Heat the oven to 350F degrees.

Char the poblanos over gas burners (or other methods available online). After you have charred the poblanos, place them in a paper bag and let them steam and cool. Rub the skins off. Make a slit in the chilies and remove the seeds. If you tear the chili, it is okay, just spread them out (trying to 'curl' the edges like a taco shell). If that does not work, do not worry, it will work uncurled too.

Cook the hamburger and onions and drain any grease. Add corn, about 1 cup cooked rice (leftover rice is perfect), cumin, ancho chili powder (if you don't have ancho, any regular chili powder will be fine), take off the heat, and add the black beans and cherry tomatoes.

Spoon about half of the meat mixture over the chilis and add some green salsa and some cubed pepper jack cheese. Cover with the remaining meat, cubed cheese, and salsa, and sprinkle some grated jack cheese over the top. Bake in the oven for 45 minutes. Sprinkle with green onions and cilantro to serve.

This is an everything-but-the-kitchen-sink kind of recipe. You can add extra rice or no rice. You can use pinto beans or kidney beans. Use cheddar cheese if you prefer or mix the two cheeses. Extra jalapeño if you like it hot, or just Hatch chilies if you are a wimp, and if you are a big wimp, none at all. You can use shrimp instead of hamburger. You can trade the green onions for a regular onion. This is a good dish to freeze. Just defrost and bake. Serves 4.

Pork and Star Anise Stew (R.I.P., Stare Decisis)

We hardly knew ye...

Ingredients

- Olive oil, for frying and drizzling
- 1 1/2 lbs. pork shoulder or Boston butt, cut into chunks (trim fat)
- 2 oz bacon, cut into strips crosswise
- 1 white onion, diced
- 2 garlic cloves, minced
- 1 1/2 T all-purpose flour
- 2 cups dry (hard) cider (I like Golden State Dry Hard Cider)
- 4 sprigs of fresh thyme
- 3 bay leaves
- 1/2 tsp dried cloves
- 2 star anise (very important ingredient for this dish)
- 1/2 tsp cinnamon
- 1 T apple cider vinegar
- 1 (about 6 oz) apple, peeled, cored, and cut into chunks
- 1 T Dijon mustard
- 1 T pure maple syrup
- Salt and freshly ground black pepper
- (1) 8 oz container crème fraiche
- Wild rice for serving

Cooking Steps

Heat the oven to 350F degrees.

Warm 1 to 2 T oil in a large oven-proof saucepan over medium heat. Working in batches to avoid crowding the meat, add the pork chunks and brown on all sides, about 6 minutes. Transfer the pork to a bowl, cover, and repeat with any remaining pork, adding oil if needed.

Add the bacon to the pan and cook until crispy. Drain the bacon and set aside. Drain most of the grease.

Stir in the onion and garlic, and cook until the onion is softened, about 5 minutes.

Sprinkle the flour over the ingredients in the pan and stir to ensure it's well incorporated into the onion mixture. Then pour in the cider. Add the vinegar, apple, thyme, bay leaves, dried cloves, star anise, cinnamon, mustard, and syrup to the saucepan.

Return the browned pork and bacon to the pan, pour in any cooking juices that accumulated in the bowl, and stir to combine.

Transfer the casserole to the oven, and cook uncovered until the pork is very tender, about 1 1/2 hours. Do not overcook. Remove from the oven and remove the star anise (be sure to 'fish' out all the star anise - you don't want to bite into it) and thyme stems. Season with salt and pepper to taste, then stir in the crème fraiche. Serve over cooked wild rice. White rice will work too. Serves 4 to 6.

Slow-Cooked Pot Roast (Cooked Using Our Favorite Tactic – Delay, Delay, Delay)

Delay is a tactical legal strategy, taken to an art form by Trump, and is assisted by the courts. Months and months to determine if a former president has absolute immunity to commit any crime while in office, including hypothetically killing his opponent? Really?

Ingredients

- 1 boneless chuck roast or 7 bone roasts (if you can find them). The idea is to use a "flat" roast.
- 1 onion, chopped
- Fresh sliced mushrooms (eyeball the amount, I use at least 12-15 mushrooms)
- Low sodium beef broth (enough to cover the meat)
- Several shakes Worcestershire sauce
- 10 sprigs fresh thyme or 1 T dried thyme
- 1 large bay leaf
- Celery seed (at least 1 tsp)
- Salt and pepper
- Flour
- Carrots (4 to 6) peeled and cut into roughly the same size but not too small
- 1 lb. fusilli noodles

Cooking Steps

Put the roast in a large pan and cover it with broth. Add chopped onions, sliced mushrooms, Worcestershire sauce, thyme, celery seed, salt and pepper, and bay leaf.

Sprinkle a little flour over the roast in the pan. I take a little bit and pinch it between my thumb and fingers. Be careful or it will lump. (You can use the standby Wondra if you are too chicken). I eyeball it...not too much. The idea is to get the broth a little thicker.

Turn to a boil, then lower to a simmer and cover the pot. Cook at least 2 hours, but longer is okay too. I turn the roast over about halfway through cooking. About an hour before you are ready to eat, add the carrots.

When the meat is done, remove it from the pan, and cover to keep warm. Bring the liquid back to a boil. You will likely need to add more broth. Once the pot is boiling, add the fusilli and cook until tender. Serve immediately. Serves 4 to 6.

Inspiration: Glen

Recipe: Shirley

White's Only Chili (Rolling Back the Voting Rights Act!)

Minority voters, you've had a good run, but it's over!

Ingredients

- 1 T olive oil
- 1 1/2 lbs. skinless, boneless chicken breast, cut into bite-sized pieces
- 1/2 tsp salt
- 1 onion, chopped
- 2 garlic cloves, minced
- 1 T cumin
- 2 tsp coriander
- 1 tsp ground oregano
- 1/4 tsp cayenne pepper (see note)
- (2) 15 1/2 oz cans of cannellini beans, rinsed and drained
- 1 can 3 1/2 oz chopped green chilis (mild or hatch), undrained (see note)
- 2 cups chicken broth, low sodium
- 12 oz beer (not lite)
- 3/4 cup grated jack cheese (or depending on your taste, pepper jack)

Cooking Steps

In a Dutch oven (soup pot) over medium heat, add the oil and chicken, stirring until no longer pink. Add the onion, garlic, cumin, coriander, oregano, and cayenne, stirring occasionally until the onion is softened, about 3-5 minutes.

Add the 2 cups of chicken broth, beer, green chilies, and 1 can of beans. Bring to a boil and reduce the heat to medium.

Mash the remaining can of beans with a fork or potato masher and add to the chili. Simmer for 30 minutes and add the cheese until it is melted.

Serve with garnishes of your choice, like cilantro leaves, lime wedges, extra grated cheese, and sour cream. Delicious with crushed tortilla chips if you want to go over the top.

Note: If you want hotter chili, you can add 1 diced jalapeño or diced poblano when adding the chilies. If you want, you can also add jalapeños as a garnish. Serves 4 to 6.

Alabama Extra White BBQ Sauce (We Like Our Sauce Like We Like Our Country!)

The Supreme Court's recipe 'in order to form a more perfect union...'

Ingredients

- 1 cup mayonnaise
- 1 1/2 T white vinegar
- 1 1/2 T apple cider vinegar
- 1 T spicy brown mustard
- 2 tsp cream-style horseradish
- 1 T brown sugar
- 1 tsp lemon juice
- 1/2 tsp finely diced poblano chilis (no seeds)
- 1 clove garlic
- 1/4 tsp jalapeño pepper salt (optional...if you can find it)
- 1/2 tsp salt
- 1/2 tsp pepper
- 1 tsp paprika

Cooking Steps

Mix all the ingredients together in a blender or food processor until smooth. Keep in a jar with a lid and refrigerate for several hours before using. Brush on chicken while grilling, or use with BBQ pork ribs, pork roast, or fish.

Can be used as a dipping sauce, especially with chicken wings. Works as salad dressing too!

Carrot Orzo (For Our Favorite Orange President)

Still exhausted from all the winning? Citizens United. Worst. Decision. Ever.

Ingredients

- 2 cups carrots, chopped in a food processor
- 1 onion, chopped
- 2 cloves garlic, minced
- 2 cups orzo
- 1 tsp salt
- 1 tsp pepper
- 2 1/2 cups chicken broth
- 2 tsp fresh thyme
- 1 cup grated parmesan cheese
- Italian parsley, chopped

Cooking Steps

Chop the carrots for about 15 seconds in the food processor until chunky and just larger than peas. Melt the butter, add carrots and onion, and cook until softened for 5 minutes. Add orzo and garlic and stir into carrots and onion mixture.

Once mixed, add in the broth and heat until boiling. Turn it down to a simmer, and cook uncovered for about 18 to 20 minutes, stirring often until the orzo is creamy and the liquid has evaporated. Stir in cheese, thyme, and parsley. You can add cooked chicken, sausage, or shrimp for a main course. Serves 6.

Spicy Brown 'Sugar Daddy' Roasted Carrots (By Harlan Crow)

Definition of a Sugar Daddy: He pays your nephew's tuition, buys your mom's home and doesn't charge her rent, and takes you on breathtaking vacations. I want one, too!

Ingredients

- 10 to 15 medium carrots (I use the colorful smaller ones, but good old orange works too)
- 1 to 2 T olive oil (just enough to lightly coat the carrots)
- 1 T dried thyme
- Salt and pepper
- 2 T soft butter
- 1/2 tsp cumin
- 1/2 tsp ground thyme
- 1/2 tsp ground coriander
- 1/2 tsp turmeric
- 1/2 tsp harissa powder (you can substitute Aleppo pepper)
- 1 1/2 T brown sugar

Cooking Steps

Heat the oven to 425F degrees.

Cut the carrots in half lengthwise and crosswise the same size and not large pieces. The larger end of the carrot may need more cuts than the tapered end, depending on the size of the carrots.

Toss the cut carrots in a bowl with the olive oil, salt, pepper, and 1 T thyme, place the carrots in one layer in an ovenproof pan (a cast iron pan is perfect), and roast in the hot oven for 20 to 25 minutes, stirring every 10 minutes.

While the carrots are roasting, mix the soft butter, brown sugar, and spices. When the carrots look close to done and are tender, add the butter mixture to the carrots, rolling the carrots until they are coated with the spice mixture. Bake for another 5 minutes. The carrots should look slightly caramelized. Serves 4.

Cold Asparagus (We Haven't Spared Mifepristone Yet. See You Back in Court, Soon!)

It looks like the Justices have learned their lesson; Women vote, and they have a memory! Who knew? Imagine the court's post-Dobbs horror; no 2022 red wave, a dismal 2023 special elections showing, continuing to lose elections in early 2024 (even in Alabama), and states enshrining abortion rights, right and left. Mifepristone will probably survive this initial 2024 Supreme Court case, but don't be tricked: it will resurface after the election, likely by way of the Comstock Act (which prevents the mailing of drugs used for abortions). After all, their mantra is "all hands on deck" for Trump and Republicans – 2024, and beyond!

"The next Republican president could effectively ban most abortions through a simple policy change at the Department of Justice, experts and advocates on both sides of the abortion debate say."

The Heritage Foundation (oh, great, now we have billionaire money involved too), which has proposed detailed policies for a potential GOP administration, argues that Comstock "unambiguously prohibits mailing abortion drugs," and says that the next administration should "enforce federal law against providers and distributors of abortion pills." (Axios)

Sorry girls, it doesn't look good!

Ingredients

- 1 lb. asparagus
- Cilantro (stemmed), the better part of a bunch, depending on your taste
- 1/2 cup soy sauce (I use light soy sauce)
- 1/4 cup toasted sesame oil
- Toasted sesame seeds

Cooking Steps

Simmer the asparagus in a water bath until tender but not overcooked. Dip immediately in an ice bath to stop the cooking. When cool, drain and cover with plastic wrap and refrigerate until ready to serve.

Make the sauce by combining the soy and sesame oil. You can make it ahead of time and refrigerate. To serve, put the asparagus in a serving dish, pour over the dressing mixture, and top with picked stemmed cilantro and toasted sesame seeds. You can increase easily and adjust the dressing per your taste... we love sesame oil, others not so much. Serves 4.

Mexican Macaroni (Keep Latinos on the Mexican Side)

After all, Mexico is going to pay for the wall, but where are the pesos?

Ingredients

- 1 lb. package elbow macaroni
- 1 onion, chopped
- (2) 14 1/2 oz cans low sodium chicken broth
- (3) 10 oz cans original Rotel Diced Tomatoes and Green Chilis (the key to this recipe)
- 16 oz container sour cream
- 1 lb. grated sharp cheddar cheese (see note)
- 1 T vegetable oil

Cooking Steps

Heat the oven to 350F degrees.

Fry macaroni in vegetable oil, stirring until lightly brown. (Careful, it burns easily.) Over medium heat, add the chopped onion to the macaroni and stir, watching that the macaroni and onion do not burn (if needed add more oil). Add Rotel tomatoes and broth, and simmer uncovered until cooked al dente and the liquids are absorbed. Add more broth if necessary to keep it moist.

In a large casserole, add half of the macaroni mixture, half of the sour cream, and half of the cheese. Repeat the layers. Bake for 45 minutes. I cover the pan for the first 30 minutes and remove the cover for the remaining 15 minutes or until it is a little bubbly. It serves 8 to 10.

This is much better than you would think. I have friends and family ask me to make it all the time. It is an excellent side dish (especially with anything BBQed) and can become a main course if you add cooked hamburger, leftover steak, or chicken.

Note: Grate your own cheese…the pre-grated cheese you buy at the market is treated with something that keeps the cheese from melting correctly.

Gunpowder Potatoes (An Original N.R.A. Recipe)

As their billionaires' gun consultants say, if you can't have a gun in your potatoes, why not gunpowder? A well-regulated militia? How about well-regulated firearms?

Ingredients

- 1 1/2 lbs. small baby new potatoes
- 1/2 tsp cumin seeds
- 1/2 tsp coriander seeds
- 1/2 tsp fennel seeds
- 1 T olive oil for brushing
- 3 T scallions, finely chopped
- 2 T chopped cilantro
- 1/2 Anaheim green chili, finely chopped (see note)
- 1/2 tsp sea salt flakes
- 3 T butter, melted
- 2 T lime juice
- 1 tsp garam masala
- 1/2 tsp cumin
- 1/2 chili powder
- 1 tsp coriander powder
- 1/2 tsp fennel pollen
- 1/4 tsp cayenne
- 1/4 tsp cinnamon

Cooking Steps

Boil a large pan of salted water. Add the potatoes and cook until just tender (12 to 15 minutes). Drain and allow to dry in a colander. Toss them in a bit of oil on a baking sheet.

Meanwhile, toast all the seeds in a hot dry frying pan for 2 minutes until fragrant. Crush in a mortar and pestle or spice blender, and add to a large bowl with the onions, cilantro, and chiles.

Spice blend: Mix the garam masala, cumin, chili powder, coriander powder, fennel pollen, cayenne, and cinnamon. Add to the bowl with the other ingredients. This spice blend is also good on chicken and shrimp before BBQing.

Broil the potatoes for 5 to 7 minutes until they are golden and crispy, turning the potatoes halfway through the cooking. Once they are out of the broiler, cut them in half so the ingredients will adhere to the potatoes.

Add the cut potatoes to the bowl with the ingredients and spices and add the melted butter and lime juice. Toss well and serve immediately.

Note: The chili choice is a matter of personal taste. I use half an Anaheim or even half of a poblano. If you like it spicier, consider a jalapeño or two. Use as a side dish with Indian food, BBQed shish kabobs, or steak. Serves 4.

Thanksgiving Stuffing (Make Stuff-Upism, a.k.a. Originalism/Textualism)

One of the court's favorite tools, to apply (and not apply) as needed to fit their ideological dogma.

Once at a restaurant in South Carolina, I saw this on the specials for the day chalkboard: Vegetable of the Day, Cornbread Stuffing. Side dish or vegetable? I'm going with side dish.

Ingredients

- 1/2 bag Pepperidge Farms Herb Seasoned Classic Dressing
- 1/2 bag Pepperidge Farms Cornbread Dressing
- 1 lb. sage sausage (breakfast sausage with sage)
- 2 large onions
- 4 stalks celery
- 15 to 20 mushrooms, depending on size. (Another gauge: I use a bag in the produce section and fill it about halfway with mushrooms. I use white mushrooms, but you can use brown mushrooms. You need a lot of mushrooms.
- Chicken broth

Cooking Steps

Put the half bags of dressing mix into a large bowl and save the remaining half bags for future use, or until you have to throw them out because moths are flying around.

Cook the sausage and drain off the grease, cool, and add to the bowl with the dressing.

Cut the onions and celery into big chunks (err on the larger size at least in 1-inch pieces). Clean the mushrooms and cut them into quarters if they are large; in halves if medium size and leave whole if they are small.

Do not pre-cook the vegetables! Add the uncooked cut onions, celery, and mushrooms into the bowl with the stuffing mix. Mix in enough chicken broth until you have a wet (not sloppy) consistency. I stuff the turkey and add a bit more broth to the unstuffed dressing that will be cooking in the oven since it tends to be drier. If you don't stuff the turkey, or for excess dressing, add some of the drippings/juices/grease to the dressing since it will not get the juices from the turkey (sounds awful I know) but adds turkey flavor to the dressing. Cook, covered, for about 1 to 1 1/2 hours in a 325F degree oven.

This is a personal taste kind of recipe. No wrong amounts of vegetables and mushrooms, just adjust to your likes and tastes.

The larger cut vegetables will be soft with a teeny, tiny crunch but won't be mushy like most other dressings, also making the dressing much easier to make. Then you can have a Bloody Mary and watch the Macy's Thanksgiving Day Parade or a football game with your family instead of slaving over the stove.

Turkey notes: I have tried every type of turkey and cooking method – big breasted, pre-basted, hormone free, free range, caged, extra white meat, fresh, and not frozen. Frozen. Organic, grain fed, grass fed. I have marinated the turkey overnight in a bag, deep fried the turkey, cooked it breast side down, BBQed it, low temperature, high temperature, you name it. My conclusion? I know this is blasphemy, but in the end they all taste the same to me. So now I buy the cheapest one! They are just as good, and no one ever complains! When I saw Sarah Palin standing in front of the turkey head grinder machine with a turkey being lowered in... I was over it!

Billionaire Shortbread Bars (Our Favorites!)

And billionaires love them! The definition of a symbiotic relationship.

Ingredients

- 12 T (1 1/2 sticks) unsalted butter, melted
- 1/2 cup granulated sugar
- 1 1/2 tsp vanilla extract
- 1 1/2 cups all-purpose flour
- 1/4 tsp kosher salt

Cooking Steps

Heat the oven to 325F degrees.

Line an 8x8 baking pan with parchment paper that hangs slightly over the edges and set aside.

In a medium bowl, mix the melted butter, granulated sugar, and vanilla. Add the flour and kosher salt, and stir just until combined, being careful not to overmix.

Press the dough evenly into the prepared baking dish. Bake until the edges are just slightly golden brown, 30 to 35 minutes. Set aside to cool while you prepare the caramel.

Caramel
- 1/2 cup granulated sugar

- 2 T Lyle's Golden Syrup (or light corn syrup)
- 1/2 cup butter
- 2 T cream
- 1 tsp salt
- 2 tsp vanilla extract

Combine the sugar and syrup in a medium saucepan. Cook on medium heat, stirring constantly until it becomes a light caramel color.

Add the butter, salt, and milk, then stir until smooth. Remove from heat and mix in the vanilla. Set aside to cool slightly, then pour over the cooled shortbread. Allow it to cool completely.

Ganache
- 9 oz 70% dark chocolate
- 3/4 cup heavy cream
- Flaky sea salt (for garnish)

Add the chocolate to a double boiler and melt. Stir in the cream and mix until smooth. Pour the ganache over the cooled caramel and spread it in an even layer with a spatula. Sprinkle with flaky sea salt and refrigerate until chilled, about 1 hour. Lift the square out of the pan using the long sides of the parchment paper. Cut the shortbread into squares and serve slightly chilled.

Chocolate Obliviousness Brownies (Better Than Letting Them Eat Cake)

Special thanks to Justice Ketanji Brown Jackson for referencing Marie Antoinette's "Let them eat cake," to describe obliviousness in her Affirmative Action dissent! In May 2024, a Marquette Law School poll found that 61% of American adults disapprove of the job the Supreme Court is doing. Quelle surprise…

Ingredients

- 8 oz excellent quality semi-sweet chocolate
- 12 T butter, melted
- 1 cup + 2 T of sugar
- 2 eggs
- 2 tsp vanilla extract
- 3/4 cup all-purpose flour
- 3/4 cup cocoa powder (do not scrimp, use good cocoa powder)
- 1 tsp salt
- 1/2 cup good quality chocolate chips
- Optional: 1/2 cup walnuts or pecans

Cooking Steps

Heat the oven to 350F degrees.

Line an 8-inch square pan with parchment paper and chop the chocolate into 70 chunks. Melt half of the chocolate in the microwave in 20-second intervals, saving the other half for later.

In a bowl, mix the butter and sugar, then add the eggs and vanilla, and mix for 1 to 2 minutes until the mixture is light and fluffy.

Whisk the melted chocolate into the bowl with the butter, sugar, and egg (make sure it is not too hot or else it will cook the eggs), then sift in the flour, cocoa powder, and salt. Fold in the dry ingredients, being careful not to overmix. Fold in the remaining chocolate chunks and chocolate chips and transfer the batter to the prepared pan.

Bake for 20 to 25 minutes, depending how fudgy you like your brownies, then cool completely.

Bananas Foster (A Fascist Republic Classic)

Fascism is when the conservative party is too small, and they can't win legitimately (a conservative's worst nightmare). A little fascism can get you over the finish line when you have zero morals.

Ingredients

- 1/4 cup butter
- 1 cup brown sugar
- 1/2 tsp cinnamon
- 1/4 cup banana liqueur
- 1/4 cup dark rum
- 4 bananas, cut lengthwise and then cut crosswise
- Vanilla ice cream

Cooking Steps

Combine the butter, brown sugar, and cinnamon in a pan and heat until melted and bubbly, but do not let it burn.

Add the bananas and cook for 2 minutes or until the bananas are softened, well-coated, and look almost caramelized.

Carefully add the banana liqueur and the rum. Stand back as the alcohol warms because it will ignite. Turn the pan a bit to the side and light with a long match. It makes a spectacular show but be careful!

Dish up four bowls of ice cream, and, once the flames are out, dish up the bananas and the warm sauce, and serve immediately. Serves 4.

Grift Gift Chocolate Fudge Sauce (Grift/Gift, What's the Diff?)

Delicious fudge sauce and a great gift. Put it in a jar with a bow; a refreshing change for the hostess inundated with jam, jelly, and chutney gifts. Good enough to buy you a Supreme Court Justice.

Ingredients

- 3 squares (3 oz) unsweetened chocolate
- 1/4 cup butter
- 1 cup confectioners' sugar
- 6 T heavy cream
- 1 tsp vanilla
- 1 to 2 T Grand Marnier (optional)

Cooking Steps

In a pan or double boiler, melt the chocolate and butter over low heat, stirring constantly with a whisk. When the chocolate is melted, beat in sugar. Add 3 T heavy cream and continue beating. When well-blended, beat in remaining cream. Add vanilla and Grand Marnier. The sauce keeps well and makes a good gift.

Recipe: Private Collection

Chocolate Mousse (June 30th – The Annual Mega F.U. Decision Day Comfort Food)

There is a pattern... the last day of the Supreme Court's term and the big FU is delivered, while the conservative justices skulk off on their billionaire-funded vacations!!

My friend's mom, Suzanne, started a small tour business to Paris when she was in her sixties, and Les Trois Moutons was always a dinner destination!

Ingredients

- 8 oz exceptionally good dark chocolate (I am a Scharffenberger girl, but any really good chocolate will do. You could also exchange some dark chocolate for bittersweet chocolate. Like 6 oz dark and 2 oz bittersweet. Or not.)
- 3 T strong coffee
- 3 egg yolks
- 4 egg whites
- 4 T butter
- 1/3 cup sugar

Cooking Steps

Beat the egg yolk with 1/3 of the sugar (keep remaining sugar for later) until very well beaten (the recipe says until almost white). Mix the yolks and cooled chocolate.

Beat the egg whites with the remaining sugar until they form peaks... firm but not dry.

Fold the egg whites into the chocolate gently. Do not over mix. Put in a serving dish or dishes. Refrigerate. Serves 8.

The secret to this recipe is there is no added whipped cream that dilutes the delicious chocolate (like many chocolate mousse recipes). Les Trois Moutons serves the mousse in a crock and as it is passed to you, you dish out your individual serving and continue passing. It is very French and unbelievably delicious.

Recipe: Suzanne's Les Trois Moutons Chocolate Mousse (1978)

Coupe Denmark (Our Favorite January 6th Coup Treat)

Getting to rule on this case is more delicious than a Hot Fudge Sundae! The immunity hearing, thanks to the conservative justices, was a doozy! The fix was in from the beginning, since the conservative justices absolutely did not want to talk about the case they are expected to rule on, so veered off into non-indictment topics like internment camps, presidents pardoning themselves, suggestions to bury, oops, I mean remand - the case back to the district court, three legged stools, and special prosecutors.

If the justice department lawyer brought up any issue pertaining to the indictment, the justices would say, "I don't want to talk about that." Seriously. The mind blower? Alito suggests that it would preserve democracy if Presidents have immunity to commit federal crimes so they don't have to worry about being sued if it is a close election. Otherwise, understandably, they might not leave their office. (Sound familiar?) This non-sequitur reasoning, even by Alito standards, is ridiculous and disturbing. Alito implies that the transfer of power over the last 248 years has always been a shaky, nail-biting, undertaking.

News flash: no incoming president has ever sued an outgoing president because of a close election; and only Trump has threatened to. Reminder, this case has to do with a president desperately attempting to overturn the will of the people to stay in power.

A Coupe Denmark, also known as a Dame Blanche, is a hot fudge sundae, served with the finest quality vanilla ice cream and hot fudge or hot chocolate in a pitcher on the side of the dish of ice cream. (The presentation is equally important.)

Vanilla Ice Cream (8 scoops), and chocolate sauce (I use the **Grift Gift Chocolate Fudge Sauce**). Or you can buy fudge sauce or make your own. Put two scoops of vanilla ice cream in a goblet. If you don't have a goblet, use a bowl or even a largish glass. Put the goblets on the table and pass the heated chocolate/fudge sauce in a pitcher and let everyone make their own Coupe Denmark. Even better if you have small individual pitchers, put an individual pitcher with each goblet.

You can serve it with whipped cream but don't get it too Jim-crackied up. For the Coupe Denmark, try and skip the fruit, nuts, cherries etc. Just enjoy the delicious ice cream and silky fudge sauce! Serves 4.

Hunter Biden Crack(er) Pie (We Love a Private Drama Addiction Case Featuring a Biden)

The last time I looked, Hunter Biden was a private citizen and had nothing to do with making or influencing our laws. Looking at you, Javanka…

Ingredients

- 20 Ritz Crackers, crumbled (soda crackers are okay too)
- 3 egg whites
- 1/2 cup brown sugar
- 1/2 cup granulated sugar
- 3/4 tsp baking powder
- 1 cup coarsely chopped pecans or walnuts
- 1 tsp vanilla
- 1/4 tsp salt

Cooking Steps

Heat the oven to 325F degrees.

Beat the egg whites until stiff and gradually add the brown and granulated sugar, salt, baking powder, and vanilla. Fold in the crackers and chopped nuts.

Pour into a 9-inch buttered pie pan and bake for 30 minutes. Serve warm, at room temperature or cold. You can top it with whipped cream, fruit, or even ice cream. You can also fold in diced dried fruit before you bake the pie… Huachuca (dried persimmons, if you are lucky enough to find them), dates, or dried cherries. This is an easy last-minute dessert to throw together if you have crackers available and guests pending. Serves 6 to 8.

Wedding Cupcakes (The LGBTQ Wedding Cake Loophole...Give Us Time)

Thanks, Supreme Court, for the two rulings affirming that we can now discriminate using "free speech or religious beliefs" to opt out of providing services based on race, religion, or other criteria, regardless of anti-discrimination laws. Bringing back discrimination, one ruling at a time!

Ingredients

- 1 cup all-purpose flour
- 1 1/2 tsp baking powder
- 1 tsp salt
- 1 cup sugar
- 4 large eggs
- 6 oz (1 1/2 sticks) unsalted butter, melted and cooled a bit but still liquid
- 1/2 cup buttermilk
- 1 vanilla bean split, and seeds removed
- Zest from 1/2 an orange

Cooking Steps

Heat the oven to 350F degrees.

Put racks in the center of the oven and line cupcake pans with paper liners.

Sift the flour, baking powder, and salt into a medium bowl and set it aside.

Fill a saucepan halfway with water and bring to a simmer over medium heat. Combine the sugar and eggs in the bowl of your standing mixer (or other large bowl) and place over the simmering water — creating a double boiler — being careful that the bottom of the bowl does not touch the water. Whisk constantly. Using a thermometer, bring the temperature to 110F degrees, about 2 to 3 minutes.

Remove from heat and use the whisk attachment of your mixer to whip at high speed for 6 to 8 minutes. The egg mixture will be pale yellow and triple the original size. Turn the mixer to medium and whisk for 2 more minutes to stabilize the batter. At low speed, slowly stream the melted butter into the batter and mix until incorporated.

Fold in 1/3 of the dry ingredients, being careful not to deflate the batter. Add 1/3 of the buttermilk and continue to fold carefully. Repeat these steps with the remaining two-thirds of these ingredients. Fold in the vanilla beans and orange zest.

Pour the batter (about 1/4 cup each) into the prepared cupcake papers, leaving about 1/4-inch at the top of each paper liner.

Bake for about 20 minutes, rotating halfway through the bake, until the tops are golden brown and spring back with the touch of your finger.

Remove from the pans and allow to completely cool before frosting and/or decorating. Makes 24 standard size cupcakes.

Dark Chocolate Frosting
- 12 oz bittersweet (64%) chocolate
- 1 1/2 cups heavy cream
- 1 T butter at room temperature

Milk Chocolate Frosting
- 12 oz milk chocolate
- 3/4 cup heavy cream
- 1 T butter at room temperature

With a serrated knife, finely chop the chocolate. Set it aside.

Bring the cream to a boil in a medium saucepan. Turn off the heat. Wait 1 minute, then add the chocolate. Wait another minute then, using a rubber spatula, slowly mix the chocolate and cream until fully incorporated. Be sure not to mix air into the ganache. When you think it is fully mixed, continue for 1 more minute. Add the butter and mix to fully incorporate.

Allow to cool until it reaches a temperature (about 70F degrees) that is right for spreading or piping onto the cupcakes.

The ganache can be made in advance and refrigerated for up to 2 weeks. Bring the ganache to room temperature before using. The frosted/decorated cupcakes can be made and refrigerated for 2 days before using. Bring them back to room temperature before serving.

This recipe is from my friend Mark, who is a fabulous pastry chef.

Clarence's Oreo Ice Cream Pie (Sorry – Not Sorry)

I couldn't help myself.

Ingredients

- 25 Oreo cookies crushed, plus an additional 1 cup crushed Oreo cookies for filling and topping
- 5 T butter
- 1 pint chocolate ice cream, softened
- 1 pint vanilla ice cream, softened
- 1 cup chocolate fudge sauce (I use the **Grift Gift Chocolate Fudge Sauce**) or substitute with your favorite chocolate sauce).

Cooking Steps

Lightly butter or spray an 8 or 9-inch pie pan and set aside.

Crush the 25 Oreos in a food processor or with a rolling pin in a plastic bag. Do not remove the crème filling. Crush and reserve enough Oreo crumbs to make 1 cup and set aside. Stir the 25 crushed Oreos together with melted butter, press into the springform pan, and freeze until firm.

Spread 1 pint softened chocolate ice cream over the Oreo layer. Smooth the top and freeze until firm. Drizzle with 1/2 cup chocolate sauce, sprinkle with 1/2 cup crushed Oreos, and freeze until firm. Repeat layer with softened vanilla ice cream, smoothing and freezing until firm. Drizzle the reserved 1/2 cup chocolate sauce and remaining crushed Oreos over the top of the pie.

Cover the pie with plastic wrap or foil and place in the freezer for at least 3 hours. Let the pie sit out of the freezer for about 10 minutes before slicing and serving.

You can change up the ice cream flavors. Use only vanilla, coffee, chocolate, or pistachio ice cream. The sky's the limit. Lots of steps but worth it. You can assemble this pie several days ahead. Serves 8.

*Bonus Recipe: 'Stop the Steal Upside-Down Flag Cake' (Martha Ann's Masterpiece)

Karen – oops! I mean Martha-Ann Alito has a job; she is in charge of the flagpole. Lowering, raising, and designing flags. Each day, she can determine the flag and flag position, based on which neighbor, or group of Americans, are currently pissing her off. Did anyone check her flagpole when Trump was found guilty on 34 felony counts?

This recipe is perfect for the neighborhood 4th of July block party, if your neighbors include you, given your family's extreme political views.

Ingredients

- Unsalted butter and flour for a 9x13 pan
- 2 cups granulated sugar
- 1 3/4 cups all-purpose flour
- 3/4 cup unsweetened natural cocoa powder (not Dutch processed)
- 1 tsp salt
- 1 1/2 tsp baking powder
- 1 1/2 tsp baking soda
- 2 large eggs, lightly beaten
- 1/2 cup canola oil
- 1 cup whole milk
- 1 tsp pure vanilla extract

- 1 cup boiling water
- 8 oz softened cream cheese (brick style)
- 1/2 cup (1 stick) softened butter
- 4 cups powdered sugar
- 2 tsp vanilla extract
- Raspberries and blueberries

Cooking Steps

Heat oven to 350F degrees. Position a rack in the center of the oven.

Lightly butter the bottom and the sides of the pan.

In the bowl of a stand mixer fitted with the whisk attachment, combine the sugar, flour, cocoa, salt, baking powder, and baking soda, mixing on low speed. Mix in the eggs, oil, milk, and vanilla.

Increase the speed to medium and beat for 2 minutes. Reduce the speed to low and mix in the water. The batter will be soupy. Pour the batter into the cake pan. Bake for 45 to 50 minutes, **or until a skewer inserted in the center comes out clean**.

Frosting: Mix the softened cream cheese, softened butter, powdered sugar, and vanilla. If the frosting is too thick, add a dash of cream.

Decorate in the pan or remove the cooled cake from the pan to a platter, and frost with the cream cheese frosting. Decorate the frosted cake with raspberries in rows for the stripes and the blueberries in the upper left corner, representing the stars.

Place the pan or platter with the cake on the table…so that the blueberries are in the bottom right corner, for the 'stop the steal' presentation! Serves 8 to 12.

Definitions With a Little Added Sarcasm

Originalism and Textualism There are two slightly different understandings of originalism. One is that the Constitution should be interpreted based on what the drafters originally intended when they wrote it. The other is that the Constitution should be based on the original meaning of the text—not necessarily what the Founders intended, but how the words they used would have been understood at the time.

"Textualism is the theory that we should interpret legal texts, including the Constitution, based on the text's ordinary meaning. A textualist ignores factors outside the text, such as the problem the law is addressing or what the law's drafters intended. But it does mean giving consideration to what the words and phrases in the text meant when a particular constitutional provision was adopted." Originalism and Textualism are favorites of this Supreme Court, unless, of course, they conflict with their conservative dogma. Like the Fourteenth Amendment, Section 3...

Stare decisis and settled law Stare decisis, "to stand by things decided," is the concept of following previous court decisions and approaching laws more methodically to maintain a less chaotic legal order. "Settled law" is a term that jurists and legal scholars use to refer to a Supreme Court precedent that is indeed binding - unless, as in the Dobbs decision, the Court chooses otherwise. Gorsuch, Kavanaugh, and Coney Barrett assured senators at their confirmation hearings that *Roe v. Wade* was off the table because of, wait for it, "settled law."

Major Questions Doctrine In 2022, the conservative court gratuitously invoked (after basically inventing) a new rule of statutory interpretation called the "major questions doctrine", which had never been legally applied in the Supreme Court's history. An example of its application is in the case of *West Virginia v. Environmental Protection Agency* (June 2020). As stated in the Court's majority opinion, "It took hold because it refers to an identifiable body of law that has developed over a series of significant cases all addressing a particular problem: agencies asserting highly consequential power beyond what Congress could reasonably be understood to have been granted."

Bottom line? The court applied the new "major questions doctrine," in a 6 to 3 ruling, to effectively protect special interest groups instead of the public's interest in clean air and water. The court's use of the major questions doctrine could end up being used to limit the capacities of every single federal agency in the future. Now instead of federal agencies asserting "consequential power," the Supreme Court will.

Fascism and Authoritarianism Definition (from Wikipedia) "Fascism is a far-right, authoritarian, ultranationalist political ideology and movement characterized by a dictatorial leader, centralized autocracy, militarism, forcible suppression of criticism or opposition, or a cult leader, which is made to create an idealized and heroic image of a glorious leader, often through unquestioning flattery and praise.

Authoritarianism commands absolute obedience to authority, characterized by rejection of democracy and the use of strong central power to preserve the political status quo, and reductions in the rule of law, separation of powers, and democratic voting." Nailed it! Sounds just like Joe Biden... (sarcasm!)

No One is Above the Law If that were only true! While the Justice Department and many Americans seem to agree with this concept, the Court has not yet sufficiently demonstrated its agreement. The wealthier and better connected a person or organization is, the more they can manipulate, delay, and rig the law; they can absolutely be above the law.

Dobbs Decision In June 2022, in a 6-to-3 ruling, the Supreme Court overruled *Roe v. Wade*, exercising its "supreme authority," eliminating the constitutional right to an abortion after almost 50 years. Invoking its favorite "originalism and textualism" lens (which assists their conservative dogma, until it doesn't), they declared that "procuring an abortion is not a fundamental constitutional right because such a right has no basis in the Constitution's text or in our Nation's history." Seriously.

Allegations abound that Alito leaked the Hobby Lobby and Dobbs decisions, but of course, a thorough "investigation" conducted by the court itself produced zip. These allegations, if true, would be a damning indictment on an institution that portrays itself as being beyond politics or influence.

There are unconfirmed reports that the conservatives on the court realized that taking the case in 2021, just months after Coney Barrett was seated on October 26, 2020, just eight days before the 2020 election (after millions had already voted), would have looked too political. In the quest for not looking overzealous and enacting a shocking reversal for their purely ideological reasons, they made the decision to wait a year, and add it to the 2022 docket.

Citizens United v. Federal Elections Commission In its controversial decision on January 1, 2010, the Court reversed long standing campaign finance restrictions regarding limitations and transparency in the funding of elections. As a result, corporations, foundations, PACs, Super PACs, 'dark money' organizations, and other groups can now spend unlimited amounts to 'buy' politicians that support their positions. The estimate of money that will be spent for advertising alone in the 2024 election is greater than $10 billion. Bummer for swing state residents who get the lion's share of the ads.

The Voting Rights Act of 1965 This act aimed to overcome legal barriers at the state and local level that prevented African Americans from exercising their rights to vote as guaranteed by the 15th Amendment of the Constitution. Insinuating that voting issues are no longer 'relevant,' multiple court cases have eroded the Act's effectiveness, while the Court's efforts with respect to gerrymandering that dilutes minority voting rights have been slow and feeble.

Student Debt Forgiveness On June 30, 2023, the Court, invoking the "major questions" doctrine, again, (a new favorite conservative 'legislative' doctrine, and believed by many to be a tool to block Biden's appointees' authority) ruled that the Secretary of Education is not allowed to "rewrite" the HEROES Act statute to the extent of canceling $430 billion in student loan principal. Overturned by the Supreme Court in *Biden v. Nebraska*, 2023. Biden's proposal for student debt relief would have cost half of the forgiven PPP money! "I was trying to provide students with $10,000 to $20,000 in relief," Biden said. "The average amount forgiven in the PPP program was $70,000." He added, "The hypocrisy is stunning." What is troubling is that the Student Debt Forgiveness program had been the target of disparagement by thirteen Congressional Republicans who benefitted from forgiveness of PPP loans they received under the CARES Act.

Juxtaposed with the proposed student debt forgiveness is the staggering fraud of the CARES Act, signed into law March 27, 2020, by President Trump. It included $300 billion in one-time cash payments to all American taxpayers, the

Paycheck Protection Program (PPP) that was a $953 billion low interest business loan program established by the United States federal government, and the Federal Pandemic Unemployment Compensation Program (FPUC). Administration of the program was established by the Trump administration. Many participated in what prosecutors are calling the largest fraud in U.S. history — the theft of hundreds of billions of dollars in taxpayer money intended to help those harmed by the coronavirus pandemic. It is estimated that $80 billion was used for cars, houses, and frivolous personal items. Of the $790 billion in PPP loans that were distributed, $757 billion has been forgiven. Approximately $90 billion to $400 billion is believed to have been stolen from the $900 billion FPUA Assistance program — at least half taken by international fraudsters. If you think Trump's business acumen and administrative skills are stellar, you might want to rethink that position.

My Personal Commentary, Opinions, and Rant

Rule of Law Definition: "A principle under which all persons, institutions, and entities are accountable to laws that are: Publicly promulgated. Equally enforced." (*unitedstatescourts.gov*) "The restriction of the arbitrary exercise of power by subordinating it to well-defined and established laws." (Oxford Languages)

If you have enough money, and a Supreme Court aggressively delaying and obfuscating a case with national importance for your benefit, you are above the law. The Justices could have heard the case, *United States vs. Donald Trump* by reaching past the Appellate Court in October when Judge Chutkan ruled that Trump did not have absolute immunity. The Justices could have heard the case in December when the special prosecutor asked them to expedite the case and bypass the appellate court since it would end up with them anyway. The Justices could have heard the case on February 6, as soon as the Court of Appeals made a unanimous concurring ruling with Judge Chutkan, instead of waiting 23 days to release a paltry one-page order. The Justices could have scheduled the oral arguments much sooner than waiting an additional 54 days (over seven weeks!) once they agreed to take the case. The Justices could have removed the stay and allowed for pretrial preparation for the case, while they 'seriously' deliberate and contemplate, with all their collective legal knowledge and expertise, the extremely complicated constitutional fundamentals of whether a president attempting to overthrow the will of the people and foment a coup, was performing his official duties. But any of those options would defeat their objective, of intentionally slowing the case down. The conservative Supreme Court majority has shredded any pretense of integrity and ethics. It is like they are delivering a big sloppy wet kiss to Trump. Again.

The court can move very quickly when it chooses. In the student debt forgiveness case, *Biden v. Nebraska*, which had originally lost in the district court, the Supreme Court initiated and granted cert (to hear the case) before judgment, bypassing the Appellate Court entirely. The court was very anxious to rule on the case and was not interested in an Appellate Court decision; they raced to make sure student debt relief was never realized. The Supreme Court majority overturned Biden's executive decision and denied 43 million Americans of relief.

In 2021, the Biden administration proposed an extension on the Trump Pandemic Moratorium on Eviction, order. This was meant to extend relief for renters still affected by the pandemic. A lawsuit was filed: *Alabama Association of Realtors, et al v. Department of Health and Human Service, et al*, to stop the extension. The case was stayed by the district court. The realtors and landlords asked for cert from the Supreme Court on August 20, bypassing the Appellate Court, and the Supreme Court took the case. **Three weeks later**, the Supreme Court delivered its decision and overturned the Pandemic Moratorium on Eviction extension, helping the realtors and landlords throw people out onto the street. (This legal scenario, parenthetically, was what the special prosecutor asked the court to do on December 11, knowing the case would end up in the Supreme Court. But yeah, no.)

Here is another example of Supreme Court speed. On December 19, 2023, Colorado disqualified Trump from the state ballot. On January 5, 2024, the Supreme Court agrees to take the case. On February 8, 2024, the court hears oral arguments, and on March 4, 2024, they decide the case in

Trump's favor. Slam, bam, thank you ma'am! Less than 3 months! When the stopwatch and ideology line up...

I'm using these examples to show that the Supreme Court can move with alacrity when it wants, and a snail's pace when it chooses to. It feels like the conservatives have joined the Trump defense team to help game the system. Once the Supreme Court announces their decision on this "extremely complex," handwringing, vapors-producing, pearl-clutching, immunity case, they will have delayed the trial anywhere from 7 to 9 months and deprived the American voter of critical information to make an informed decision. Justice delayed is justice denied, as the old saying goes...

Thomas' not recusing from the case, which has his wife's fingerprints all over it, is blatant shameless behavior, but emblematic of his shocking display of contempt for ethics and principles. It also underscores that the court can do whatever it wants, with impunity and with zero consequences and no recourse from any entity. I guess we can surmise that Supreme Court Justices' spouses have absolute immunity from the law too. No wonder Trump calls the SCOTUS six "his judges." If the court eventually comes down with a 'bench slap' decision that (cough cough) 'no one is above the law,' the Supreme Court's delay of the criminal trial has effectively put Trump above the law. We are a divided country in a brass-knuckle national fight for political power, and the Supreme Court plays too big of a role. This is a MAGA court.

What I find particularly troubling is by purposely delaying a trial, the court will reinforce the illusion of innocence to the MAGA crowd, who already think the insurrection was a "deep state" hoax. Without a trial or evidence to the contrary, the insurrection will remain a "peaceful protest" myth. So, imagine this scenario: no trial, no clarity, and the MAGA cult (thanks to the court inaction), more convinced and energized that Trump is innocent. And then he loses? 2020 will be predictive of what's to come. Trump will spew the same false narrative that he was the winner, and the election was rigged and stolen (amplified by his congressional minions now off the insurrection hook thanks to the Supreme Court in their Colorado decision). Anything less than a peaceful transfer of power is unacceptable undemocratic behavior that will be tacitly abetted by the court, again. Same script, but I think the level of rage and violence will be even more intense. I hope I am wrong!

Remember *Bush v. Gore*, 2000? The Supreme Court stopped the vote count and handed the election to Bush. In *United States of America v. Donald Trump* in 2024, the Supreme Court is trying to stop the trial to hand the election to Donald Trump. Shocked?

If you were uncertain that the Supreme Court was political and you questioned my premise that the court places ideology above the law, I hope I have helped assuage your doubt.

Let me end the rant by finishing where I started at the beginning of this cookbook: Never forget that when you vote, you are choosing a president who will choose nominees to fill any Supreme Court vacancies that occur during his or her term. Depending on whom they appoint, there is a potential for undemocratic, unethical, and reprehensible consequences that can last for decades. Carefully consider that equation when you vote.

Made in the USA
Las Vegas, NV
23 July 2024

92808255R00089